Urs Trinkner

Regulating the Mail Market

Urs Trinkner

Regulating the Mail Market

Main Regulatory Challenges in light of Universal Service Provision, Competition, and E- Substitution

Südwestdeutscher Verlag für Hochschulschriften

Impressum/Imprint (nur für Deutschland/ only for Germany)
Bibliografische Information der Deutschen Nationalbibliothek: Die Deutsche Nationalbibliothek verzeichnet diese Publikation in der Deutschen Nationalbibliografie; detaillierte bibliografische Daten sind im Internet über http://dnb.d-nb.de abrufbar.

Alle in diesem Buch genannten Marken und Produktnamen unterliegen warenzeichen-, marken- oder patentrechtlichem Schutz bzw. sind Warenzeichen oder eingetragene Warenzeichen der jeweiligen Inhaber. Die Wiedergabe von Marken, Produktnamen, Gebrauchsnamen, Handelsnamen, Warenbezeichnungen u.s.w. in diesem Werk berechtigt auch ohne besondere Kennzeichnung nicht zu der Annahme, dass solche Namen im Sinne der Warenzeichen- und Markenschutzgesetzgebung als frei zu betrachten wären und daher von jedermann benutzt werden dürften.

Verlag: Südwestdeutscher Verlag für Hochschulschriften Aktiengesellschaft & Co. KG
Dudweiler Landstr. 99, 66123 Saarbrücken, Deutschland
Telefon +49 681 37 20 271-1, Telefax +49 681 37 20 271-0, Email: info@svh-verlag.de
Zugl.: Zurich, University of Zurich, Dissertation, 2007

Herstellung in Deutschland:
Schaltungsdienst Lange o.H.G., Berlin
Books on Demand GmbH, Norderstedt
Reha GmbH, Saarbrücken
Amazon Distribution GmbH, Leipzig
ISBN: 978-3-8381-0788-2

Imprint (only for USA, GB)
Bibliographic information published by the Deutsche Nationalbibliothek: The Deutsche Nationalbibliothek lists this publication in the Deutsche Nationalbibliografie; detailed bibliographic data are available in the Internet at http://dnb.d-nb.de.

Any brand names and product names mentioned in this book are subject to trademark, brand or patent protection and are trademarks or registered trademarks of their respective holders. The use of brand names, product names, common names, trade names, product descriptions etc. even without a particular marking in this works is in no way to be construed to mean that such names may be regarded as unrestricted in respect of trademark and brand protection legislation and could thus be used by anyone.

Publisher:
Südwestdeutscher Verlag für Hochschulschriften Aktiengesellschaft & Co. KG
Dudweiler Landstr. 99, 66123 Saarbrücken, Germany
Phone +49 681 37 20 271-1, Fax +49 681 37 20 271-0, Email: info@svh-verlag.de

Copyright © 2009 by the author and Südwestdeutscher Verlag für Hochschulschriften
Aktiengesellschaft & Co. KG and licensors
All rights reserved. Saarbrücken 2009

Printed in the U.S.A.
Printed in the U.K. by (see last page)
ISBN: 978-3-8381-0788-2

Acknowledgements

Several people have made this dissertation possible.

First and foremost, I would like to thank my advisor Prof. Dr. Helmut M. Dietl for continuing great support throughout the process of writing this dissertation. Similarly, my second adviser Prof. Dr. Dr. Matthias Finger was always there for help and valuable discussions when needed.

Since I started my research in 2003 I had the pleasure to work with several gifted economists on a number of different topics. In particular I would like to thank Dr. Christian Jaag, Dr. Mehdi Farsi, Prof. Dr. Massimo Filippini, Reto Bleisch and Dr. Martin Grossmann for their great collaboration. This research resulted in a number of papers that have been edited by Prof. Dr. Michael A. Crew and Prof. Dr. Paul R. Kleindorfer. I thank them for their very valuable comments. Further support provided Dr. Boris Krey, Dr. Stefan Saladin and Dr. Heikki Nikali (Chapter 2 of the book), Dr. Tariq Hasan, Dr. Daniel Rudis and Prof. Dr. Reto Föllmi (Chapter 4), Beat Friedli, Dr. Catia Felisberto and Prof. Dr. Panzar (Chapter 5). Moreover I thank Carsten Karkowski, Dr. Martin Lutzenberger, Dr. Andreas Grütter, Dr. Markus Lang and Dr. Stephan Werner for a great time at the Chair of Prof. Dr. Helmut M. Dietl.

Swiss Post enabled this research by supplying resources, data, and a great amount of freedom over research topics. In particular I would like to thank Dr. Stefano di Renzo, Dr. Peter Beck, Lukas Bruhin and Reto Müllhaupt for their continuing and motivating support. Please note that the views and opinions expressed in this book are mine and do not reflect those of Swiss Post.

Last but not least I thank Marie-Anne, my family and my friends for their great support.

Zurich, September 2008   Urs Trinkner

The Faculty of Economics, Business Administration and Information Technology of the University of Zurich herewith permits the publication of the aforementioned dissertation without expressing any opinion on its views.

Zurich, December 5, 2007

The Dean: Prof. Dr. H. P. Wehrli

Contents

Acknowledgements 1
1. **Introduction** 5
    1.1 Background and problem set 5
    1.2 Outline of the book 7
2. **Drivers of Mail Demand, E-Substitution, and Forecasting** 9
    2.1 Introduction 9
    2.2 Data 11
    2.3 E-Substitution in time series analysis 13
    2.4 Long run models for Swiss mail demand 15
    2.5 Forecasting future mail demand 19
    2.6 Conclusions 22
3. **Economies of Scale, Density and Scope in Mail Delivery** 25
    3.1 Introduction 25
    3.2 Background 27
    3.3 Model specification an econometric methods 28
    3.4 Data 30
    3.5 Estimation results 31
    3.6 Economies of scale, density and scope 32
    3.7 Conclusions 34
    3.8 Discussion: Mail delivery as a *contested* natural monopoly 35
4. **Overall Welfare Impact of Various Scenarios of Liberalization** 39
    4.1 Introduction 39
    4.2 Basic model and formal results 40
        4.2.1. Modeling competition in postal markets 41
        4.2.2. Model specification 42
        4.2.3. Regulated Competition with Swiss licensing system 44
        4.2.4. Licensing fees lead to higher prices 45
    4.3 Calibration with Swiss Data 46
        4.3.1. Demand parameters 46
        4.3.2. Cost structure 48

  4.4 Results on Monopoly and on End-to-End Competition 49

    4.4.1. Monopoly: Positive effects of a price freeze 50

    4.4.2. End-to-end Competition: universal service at risk 51

    4.4.3. Ambiguous effects of the licensing rate μ 53

    4.4.4. Comparison of the four regulatory regimes and first conclusions 54

  4.5 Worksharing and Price Freeze Competition 55

    4.5.1. Modeling Worksharing 56

    4.5.2. US Worksharing – a Pareto Improvement 57

    4.5.3. Price Freeze Competition 59

    4.5.4. Discussion 60

  4.6 Access with Bypass 61

  4.7 Conclusions 63

5. **Pricing in Liberalized Two-Sided Mail Markets** **65**

  5.1 Introduction 65

  5.2 Background – is the postal market two-sided? 67

    5.2.1. Pricing structures in two-sided markets 68

    5.2.2. Two-sidedness of the postal market 69

  5.3 A two-sided postal market model 70

    5.3.1. Upstream competition in non-discriminatory linear tariffs 74

    5.3.2. Downstream competition in two-part tariffs 75

  5.4 Simulation results and discussion 76

  5.5 Conclusions 80

6. **Concluding Remarks** **82**

  6.1 Two conflicting concepts: Universal Service and Free Market 82

  6.2 Impact of a Full Market Opening on Welfare 84

Abbreviations **86**

List of Tables **88**

List of Figures **89**

References **90**

1. Introduction

1.1 Background and problem set

The postal reform of Switzerland in 1998 marked the beginning of the liberalization process of the Swiss postal market[1]. Against the background of the liberalization of network industries in the European Union (EU), the former public undertaking PTT was split up into the two public enterprises Swiss Post and Swisscom, the latter being corporatized. Thereby, the postal monopoly that had lasted for more than 150 years was reduced[2] and assigned to Swiss Post. Swiss Post was in turn obliged to take over public missions, namely the universal provision in Switzerland with postal services and payment services.

It is important to note that now – in contrast to the past[3] – the postal monopoly was primarily legitimated as a means to finance universal services. Consequently, and in the light of the developments in the European postal market, the new postal act empowered the government to reduce the monopoly if the financing of universal services remained guaranteed. In 2002, the parliament approved the government's vision on a further partial market opening[4]. Accordingly, the parcels market was completely liberalized in 2004, and the letters market for addressed mail weighing more than 100 grams was opened to competition in 2006[5]. Meanwhile, the government is about to completely revise the postal law. The main issues are the possible complete liberalization of the postal market (i.e. abolishment of Swiss Post's residual monopoly), the definition of universal services and its financing, the regulatory framework, and the corporatization of Swiss Post[6].

---

[1] Postal Law and Postal Organization Act as of 1998.

[2] The monopoly was abolished for outbound mail, express, and parcels weighting more than 2kg.

[3] In the past, reserved services have primarily been justified to avoid inefficient duplication of infrastructures (see Knieps 2005 for an overview) and for reasons of national security. Further, many states regarded postal services as a means to collect taxes. Even Adam Smith (1776) considered postal services as a legitimate public business to improve the finances of the state. Interestingly, up to the First World War (introduction of income tax) the primary income of the Swiss state was customs and postal profits.

[4] "Gesamtschau zur weiteren Entwicklung des Postwesens in der Schweiz – Bericht des Bundesrates und Botschaft über die Änderung des Postorganisationsgesetzes", Mai 2002.

[5] Based on an evaluation commissioned by PostReg (WIK 2005).

[6] Press Release of the federal Department of the Environment, Transport, Energy and Communications (DETEC) as of 3rd Mai 2006 and subsequent decisions.

The current postal act reduces the complex question of liberalization to mainly one dimension, namely whether the financing of the universal service remains ensured. By suppressing political issues, this question is quickly answered from a purely economic view: The monopoly can be abolished, if either

- non-binding universal service constraints are imposed, i.e. there is no need for a financing instrument because universal services are provided by the market, or
- there exist other suitable financing instruments such as government subsidies, compensation funds, or "pay or play" mechanisms[7]. Thereby, in particular government subsidies are a powerful tool, as it is possible to finance virtually any desired level of universal services by accordingly stressing the tax payers' wallet. Technically, subsidies are even more powerful than reserved services, as the latter's upper limit is given by the profit maximizing monopoly price, while tax revenues are restricted by the Laffer effect only[8].

Thus, from a descriptive and economic point of view one can say: "There is no need for a postal monopoly to finance postal universal services". The most prominent ambassador of this standpoint is the European Commission itself. Based on comprehensive studies on the above question[9] and aiming for a full market opening, the Commission published a heavily debated proposal for a full market opening in 2009[10]. In 2008, the European Parliament and Council finally approved an amendment of the postal directive[11] that will abolish reserved services in the EC (European Communities) completely by 2011 or 2013[12]. Hence, the European member states will be forced to

---

[7] Cf. Oxera (2007) for a comprehensive overview and discussion on financing instruments. Public procurements are not to be considered as a financing instrument as they are a means to determine the cost of USO by the market (which needs to be financed somehow).

[8] Needless to say, this is a purely economic argument without any reference to its political feasibility.

[9] Cf. PWC(2006), WIK (2004, 2006), ecorys (2005). Note that none of these studies assesses the welfare consequences of a full market opening. The only prospective approach is found PWC (2006). The study analyzes the impact of a full market opening on the incumbents balance to finance for various levels of universal service constraints. The authors conclude, that a full market opening is "feasible" provided that Universal Services are properly defined ("adapted to the market") and flanking measures are available.

[10] European Commission, COM (2006) 594, Proposal for a Directive of the European Parliament and of the Council amending Directive 97/67/EC concerning the full accomplishment of the internal market of Community postal services.

[11] Directive 2008/6/EC of the European Parliament and of the Council amending Directive 97/67/EC concerning the full accomplishment of the internal market of Community postal services. Cf. Trinkner (2008) for a discussion of the Directive.

[12] Two additional years for the new member states, Luxembourg, and Greece.

finance their universal services by other means than reserved areas. Compared to the European member states, all possible financing instruments remain on the table in Switzerland which is not bound by European Directives[13].

From an economic point of view, compared to the financing question as raised above, there is a far more important and complex set of questions to be answered: What is the *welfare maximizing* regulation of the Swiss letters market? *Should* we liberalize the letters market completely, and if so, *how*?

To answer these questions, we propose a two-step approach. In a first step, Switzerland has to define the level of universal service it wants to provide to its economy. In a second step, given this definition of universal service, it is possible to evaluate the various financing means including corresponding market regimes in terms of efficiency and overall welfare. The financing means with the best combination of (a) static and dynamic effects on overall welfare and (b) risk of potential system failure is economically the one to prefer over the other ones.

For the case of Switzerland, there is little research available for both sets of questions. The main research questions addressed by this book are in the broad field of the second step. We focus on the key issue, whether a full market opening of the Swiss letters market is economically desirable given the current level of universal service obligations in Switzerland.

1.2 Outline of the book

The book builds mainly on four papers which have been published by the author between 2005 and 2008. The book provides a synthesis of this previous work and punctually deepens selected issues. Nevertheless the individual chapters can be read independently from each other.

Chapter 2 focuses on the demand side of the postal market and analyzes the drivers of Swiss mail volumes by applying time-series analysis. In particular, we compute price-elasticities and assess whether e-substitution was present in the past. E-substitution is key in postal operator's strategic planning and also affects innovation incentives in

---

[13] Technically, the European aim of harmonization of the internal market was in Switzerland already reached in 1849, when the former cantonal postal administrations were merged in the federal administration PTT. Cf. Finger (2004) for an historical overview for Swiss Post's (and PTT's) development.

monopolized mail markets. Based on the results we provide forecasts of future mail demand.[14]

Chapter 3 deepens selected issues on the supply side of the postal market. It provides an over-view on the postal value chain and focuses on the economics on mail delivery. Using econometrical cross-section methods, we compute economies of scale, density and scope. These are crucial for the economic costs of a duplication of distribution networks. We further discuss the issue of the contestability of the postal market and whether mail delivery hast to be considered a natural monopoly.[15]

Chapter 4 presents the core of the book, a game-theoretic entry model of the Swiss letters market. It aims at comparing the welfare effects of a full market opening compared to Switzerland's current residual monopoly as well as "worksharing", the current US regulatory framework. We further discuss the main findings of the literature on access with bypass and draw our conclusions.[16]

Chapter 5 analyzes optimal pricing strategies in letters markets. In particular, we focus on the question whether postal operators should charge receivers too. This leads us to the important question, whether postal markets are two-sided. If so, this would draw important implications for postal operators and regulatory authorities.[17]

We add our concluding remarks in Chapter 6. We highlight the natural conflict between universal service obligations and full market opening. Finally we summarize our results among the various chapters on the question whether the Swiss Mail market should be liberalized completely from an overall welfare point of view.

---

[14] Chapter bases on Trinkner and Grossmann (2006).
[15] Chapter bases on Farsi, Filippini and Trinkner (2006).
[16] Chapter bases on Dietl, Trinkner and Bleisch (2005).
[17] Chapter bases on Jaag and Trinkner (2008a). We also give a brief overview on the findings in Felisberto, Finger, Friedli, Krähenbühl, and Trinkner (2006) and Friedli, Jaag, Krähenbühl, Nielsen, Pihl and Trinkner (2006).

2. Drivers of Mail Demand, E-Substitution, and Forecasting

2.1 Introduction

The demand for mail is facing a great challenge. In recent years, substitutes such as e-mail and SMS (Short Message Service) have become a cheap, fast and convenient alternative. In the near future, new broadband-based services, the breakthrough of digital signatures, fully Web-based payment systems, and contracting solutions will further affect the mailing industry. In Switzerland, total addressed mail peaked in the last quarter of 2000, as shown in Figure 1 and Figure 2. Since then, mail volumes have been declining. Yet it is not clear whether e-substitution has been the underlying cause or whether this was due to some other factor such as the economic slowdown in Switzerland between 2001 and 2003.

Figure 1: Historical development of addressed mail items in Switzerland

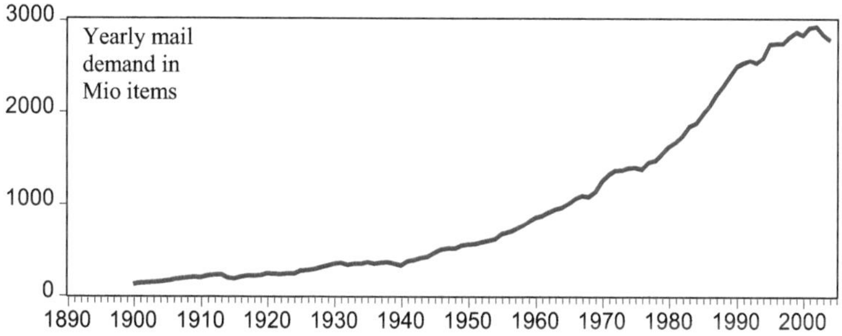

Source: Swiss Post

It is likely that e-substitution has the potential to change the long run trends of mail demand. In the past, in many countries, gross domestic product (GDP) could explain a large amount of the variation in mail demand. More recently, countries like the US, Finland[18], Sweden and the Netherlands reported that GDP is a less accurate predictor of first class mail streams. Nader (2004) concludes in his study of mail trends that "GDP and, more generally, economic activity is no longer as strong a determinant of mail volume as in the past."

---
[18] See Heikki (1997) for early E-Substitution analysis for Finland.

Figure 2: Quarterly mail demand (seasonally adjusted)

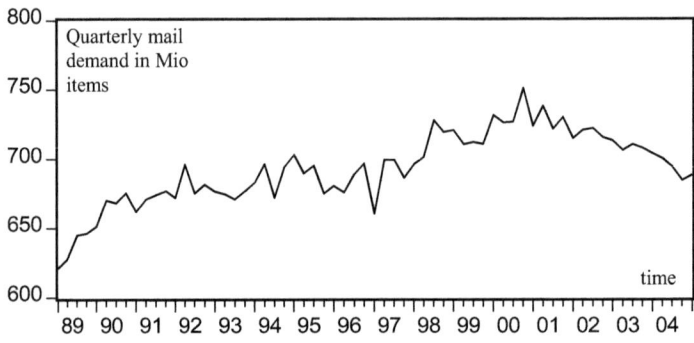

A "quick and dirt" regression with historical mail drivers underpins Nader's conclusion also for the Swiss case. Figure 3 presents the residuals of a static OLS regression of Swiss mail volumes with only income (GDP) and price as explanatory variables.[19] The test statistics indicate the existence of an omitted variable.

Figure 3: Residuals of static OLS regression, R2=97%, DW=0.57

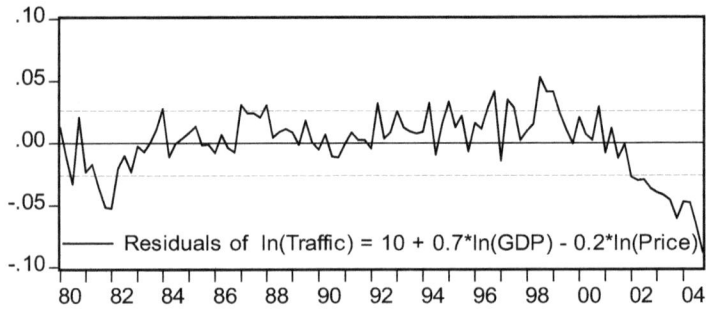

Note the autocorrelation at the end of the estimation period. The graph reveals a negative trend for the residuals after 1998. In other words, the model increasingly overestimates total traffic – a sign of e-substitution?

To get better insights about the e-substitution case in Switzerland we first look to the past. Using econometric modeling techniques, we analyze historical mail volume

---

[19] The regression is not spurious, as the three $I(1)$ variables are cointegrated.

movements to identify trends and trend-breaks. Many authors have conducted such econometric studies previously. A brief summary can be found in Cazals et al. (2003) or Harding (2004). We use time-series of aggregate mail data and apply a vector error correction model similar to the ones of Nankervis et al. (1995, 1999, 2002) and Florens et al. (2002). Other studies on aggregate data include Nikali (1997, 1998) and Pimenta et. al (1999).

We base our analysis on Trinkner and Grossmann (2006) and proceed as follows: In Section 2.2, we introduce the data. Section 2.3 deals with possible revelations of e-substitution in time series analysis. Section 2.4 presents the applied error correction models including estimation results. Section 2.5 deals with forecasting. We summarize and conclude in Section 2.6.

2.2 Data

Probably all postal services assume that the various mail streams are affected in different ways by e-substitution. However, to analyze possible trend-breaks, we need long time series on mail demand. Unfortunately, such an extensive time series does not exist on individual mail streams in Switzerland. After Swiss Post introduced fast and slow mail in 1991, no distinction between mass mail and single-piece mail has been reported until 1996. Therefore, we need to analyze aggregated mail volumes in order to get a sufficiently long time series. Aggregated mail, hereafter referred to as "total traffic," includes first and second-class mail, but not unaddressed and registered mail.

We analyzed quarterly data from 1980Q1 to 2004Q4. The main characteristics are summarized in Table 1. The last column contains the order of integration, according to the Augmented Dickey-Fuller unit root procedure.[20] Later, the order of integration will play an important role in setting up an error correction model. Traffic, GDP and all price indices are $I(1)$. Thus, the series are nonstationary, whereas their first differences $\Delta X_t = X_t - X_{t-1}$ are stationary. All the proxies for e-substitution are either $I(0)$ or $I(2)$.[21]

In the quarterly data set, the average growth in total traffic Q was about 1.7% per year. The growth rate between 1980 and 1990 was 4.1%, substantially larger than in the following decade (+1.4%). From 2000 on, the growth rate was negative (-0.9% per year).

---

[20] Discussion of the theory underlying unit roots, cointegration, and tests for them, can be found in Florens (2002) or Hamilton (1994).
[21] Similar to those in Nankervis et al. (2002), the results of the unit root test for the e-proxies should be treated with caution. Some of the series start late in the data set, and some are interpolated with only a few observations.

For real and nominal *GDP*, we observe a similar trend-break in the early 1990s, when Switzerland entered a recession followed by a period of low growth. GDP can be interpreted either as income or as economic activity reflecting a need for printed communication. The 'mail price index', *P*, reflects the price of a constant basket of various mail items of total traffic. The *CPI* (consumer price index) is issued by the Swiss National Bank. We use it to compute real measures and to account for inflation when regressing in nominal terms.

Table 1: Overview of quarterly data set

Time series (in brackets shortcuts)	Data source	Average growth rate p.y.	Period of original data	Order of integration
Traffic and GDP				
Total Traffic (Q)	Swiss Post	1.7	1980Q1 – 2004Q4	I(1)
GDP nominal	SNB	3.9	1980Q1 – 2004Q4	I(1)
GDP real (*GDP*)	SNB	1.4	1980Q1 – 2004Q4	I(1)
Price indexes				
Mail price index real (*P*)	Swiss Post	1.3***	1980Q1 – 2004Q4	I(1)
Substitutes price index (*PS*)	BACOM	0.0	1993M5 – 2004M12	I(1)
Consumer price index (*CPI*)	SNB	2.5	1980Q1 – 2004Q4	I(1)/I(2)*
Substitution proxies				
% Active e-bankers (*eBank*)	Swiss Post		1998m9 – 2004m12	I(0)
% Internet users (*eUse*)	BFS		1994 – 2004	I(2)
% Internet buyers** (*eBuy*)	BFS		2000 – 2004	I(0)
% Broadband access** (*eBb*)	BFS		1999 – 2004	I(0)
% Overall e-index (*eIndex*)	Calculated		(artificial)	I(2)
% Mobile users (*mUse*)	BACOM		1991 – 2004	I(2)
Dummies and other				
dAB		Reflects the introduction of A- and B Post in 1991		
nDays		Deviation of number of labor days from their mean		

* I(2) due to Augmented Dickey-Fuller test, I(1) with Dickey-Fuller and Phillips-Perron tests.
** These series have been extrapolated with just a few datapoints.
*** The increase in real prices was mainly due to the introduction of first class mail and the abolishment of cross-subsidies from telecommunications products.

The Swiss ministry for telecommunications has computed the telecommunication price index since 1993. We will call it the 'price of the substitute' (*PS*). It is a mixed index of telecommunications products including broadband Internet access prices. The series *PS* peaks in 1995 and is followed by a steady decline until 2000. Possible reasons for the decline are the various technological innovations and/or market liberalization. Important to us, the index reflects that substitutes, such as the Internet, e-mail, and SMS, became cheaper over time. However, properties of e-substitution other than price are hardly captured by *PS*. Table 1 does not list any variable for quality of service. We do not expect this variable to be a crucial point for our study because quality was never an issue in Switzerland.

We did not include the substitute's price *PS* in the introductory regression. A modified static regression of the kind

$$\ln(Q) = \beta_0 + \beta_1 \ln(GDP) + \beta_2 \ln(P) + \beta_3 \ln(PS) \qquad (1)$$

reveals residuals similar to the ones in Figure 3. The main difference is that the negative trend of the residuals starts in 2000 instead of 1998. We treat this as an indication that the *PS* may not sufficiently reflect the various product innovations and increasing positive network externalities of all kinds of e-substitutes. As e-substitution cannot be measured directly, we use a set of proxy variables. Loosely speaking, a proxy is a series that is somehow related to an unavailable explanatory variable for which we would like to control (in our case for e-substitution).

Table 1 lists the proxies used in our analysis. 'Active E-Bankers' (*eBank*) contains the fraction of customers who actively use Swiss Post's E-Banking platform "Yellownet".[22] The data is available on a monthly basis. It is by far the most accurate measured proxy variable because the others are available on a semiannual basis at best, creating a need for extrapolation. Interestingly, *eBank* exhibits a constant linear trend in contrast to the other e-series, which are S-shaped (e.g., the cumulative normal distribution). The only semiannual series is the fraction of active Internet users in Switzerland (*eUse*). 'Internet Buyers' (*eBuy*) contains the percentage of the Swiss population that has used the Internet to buy goods. The data was collected on a yearly basis. The series start in 2000 with a high initial value of 23%. Because the available values have been close to the ones of eUse, we adjusted the series accordingly. The series *eBb* measures the percentage of the population with a broadband connection to access e-substitutes. Finally, the overall Index (*eIndex*) was constructed as the sum of the preceding series. The last variable *mUse* contains the fraction of the population with a mobile telephone. The proxy may reflect the substitution of mail through SMS.

2.3 E-Substitution in time series analysis

E-substitution can reveal itself in various ways when performing time series analysis. A first form we encountered in Figure 3 where the plot revealed a negative trend for the residuals at the end of the estimation period. E-substitution is a straightforward

---

[22] http://www.postfinance.ch

explanation for this negative trend, as the e-proxies are highly significant when regressed against the residuals. A second and yet related indication for e-substitution could be that we cannot find a robust model over the whole time horizon without using any proxy for e-substitution.

If a model is estimated in natural logarithms, demand exhibits constant price elasticity. In equation (1), it equals parameter β_2 and is independent of Q and time. However, despite the legal monopoly of Swiss Post in the letter market, competition between physical mail and various electronic forms of written communication, such as e-mail, has evolved. In other words, one could expect increasing price elasticity and decreasing cross-price elasticity of mail demand over time. Therefore, a third way to detect e-substitution may be the estimation of model (1) over various time horizons. If price elasticity is consistently larger for samples closer to 2004, this may be a sign of e-substitution. Figure 4 shows the recursive estimates of equation (1) when the parameter for GDP (β_1) is restricted to 0.7 for all sample periods. The dotted lines represent +/- 2 standard errors[23]. 'Recursive estimates' is a procedure, in which the same equation is re-estimated for increasingly larger samples. For example, the first dot represents the estimate with a sample period from 1980Q1 to 1986Q1, whereas the last estimate has a sample period from 1980Q1 to 2004Q4. When moving to the right on the curves, the confidence bounds converge closer to the point estimates, because more observations are included in the respective estimation sample.

Figure 4: Recursive estimates yield increasing price elasticity

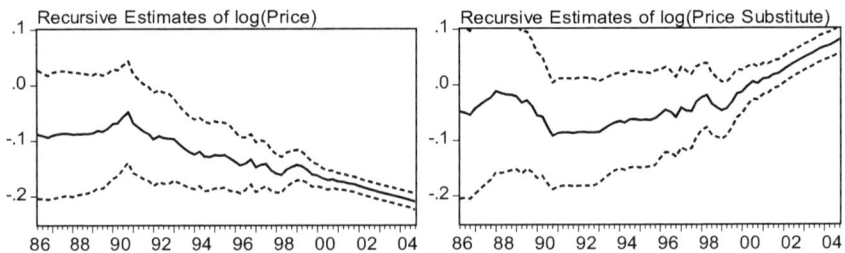

The depicted trends are in line with economic theory. With increasing competition between letters and the substitutes, prices become more important; customers get more

---

[23] A coefficient is significantly different from zero at the 95% confidence level if zero is outside the boundary.

price sensitive (price elasticity grows from -0.1 to about -0.2) and cross-price elasticity becomes significantly different from zero after 2002.

However, one of our objectives in this study is to forecast mail volumes in the near future. To do so, we need to find a robust model. This implies that it is not sufficient just to know that price elasticity may further increase over time.

2.4 Long run models for Swiss mail demand

To forecast future mail demand it would be useful to know that the relation between mail demand, real GDP, and various other factors, such as price, availability, and quality of mail and its substitutes is stable. In the previous section we saw that all of the important variables are nonstationary $I(1)$ series. According to econometric theory, a long-run equilibrium relationship may exist for nonstationary series if they are cointegrated, i.e., that a stationary linear combination of the variables is $I(0)$. Under such conditions, a so-called (vector) error correction model (VEC) gives efficient estimates. In a VEC, the cointegrated series enter in levels.[24] The name stems from the underlying error correction mechanism shifting the equilibrium variables back to their long-run equilibrium.

We will estimate three models. The 'traditional model' does not include any of the e-proxies, whereas the two 'substitution models' do. This is the only distinction between the models. We specify for all models the same long-run dynamics such that mail demand, real GDP, and prices of mail and its substitutes represent a long-run equilibrium relationship. The Johansen Cointegration test in Table 2 indicates one cointegrating relation for all three models. If the test is performed for the four endogenous series alone, it reveals one cointegrating relation as well. We chose four lags, L, to include one year with our quarterly data.

The functional form of the VEC that corresponds to Table 2 is, for Q,

$$\Delta q_t = \alpha \overbrace{(1 \cdot q_{t-1} - \beta_0 - \beta_1 gdp_{t-1} - \beta_2 p_{t-1} - \beta_3 ps_{t-1})}^{\text{Error Correction Term}} + \\ \gamma_0 + \gamma_1 dAB_t + \gamma_2 eproxy_t + \\ \sum_L \left(\gamma_{3,L} \Delta q_{t-L} + \gamma_{4,L} \Delta gdp_{t-L} + \gamma_{5,L} \Delta p_{t-L} + \gamma_{6,L} \Delta ps_{t-L} \right) + \varepsilon_t. \qquad (2)$$

---

[24] If cointegration was not found, a model in first differences would have to be specified to avoid spurious regression.

We find the cointegrating relationship in the error correction term. If it equals 0 at some time t, we have been exactly in the long-run equilibrium in the previous period t-1 (i.e., the error term ε_{t-1} was 0). If the error correction term is nonzero, it will influence the latest prediction according to the speed of adjustment α.

Table 2: Unrestricted cointegration rank test

	Traditional model		**Substitution model 1**		**Substitution model 2**	
Endogenous variables	Q, GDP, P, PS in natural logarithms		Q, GDP, P, PS in natural logarithms		Q, GDP, P, PS in natural logarithms	
Exogenous variables	dAB		dAB, $iBank$		dAB, $iUse$	
Cointegration specification	VAR and EC with constant, no trend		VAR and EC with constant, no trend		VAR and EC with constant, no trend	
Lags of VEC	4		4		4	
Johansen Cointegration test						
Null hypothesis H$_0$	Trace	Max E-V	Trace	Max E-V	Trace	Max E-V
0 cointegration relation	65.36*	27.58*	56.74*	38.43*	57.56*	36.27*
1 cointegration relation	21.12	21.13	18.30	10.63	21.28	16.01
2 cointegration relation	1.604	14.26	7.67	7.28	5.26	4.73
*Denotes 1 cointegrating relationship at 95% confidence level						

The only formal distinction between the three models lies in the choice of $eproxy_t$. In the traditional model, the term is not included at all. In the substitution models, the choice for $eproxy$ will be $eBank$ in Model 1, and $eUse$ in Model 2.

Table 3 lists the results obtained from Johansen's two-step procedure. First, the long-run equation (the error correction term in (2)) is estimated. Thereby, the parameter of q is normalized to one. In a second step, the remaining parameters in equation (2) are computed.[25]

---

[25] We used Eviews for our computations in which the procedure is implemented.

Table 3: Estimation results (Dependent variable: overall mail volume)

Adj. sample size: 1982Q2 to 2004Q4		Traditional model	E-substitution model 1	E-substitution model 2
Long run equilibrium equation				
gdp (real)		1.09 [8.14]	1.10 [9.09]	1.12 [9.58]
p (real)		-0.27 [-4.12]	-0.27 [-4.52]	-0.22 [-3.53]
ps		0.17 [4.49]	0.05 [0.60]	-0.07 [-0.57]
Constant (β_0)		1.49	1.33	1.29
Short run equation				
A		0.19 [3.98]	0.13 [2.46]	0.12 [2.03]
dAB		0.00 [0.25]	-0.01 [-0.64]	-0.01 [-0.63]
eBank			-0.21 [-4.80]	
eUse				-0.09 [-4.42]
Δq	t-1	-0.69 [-6.38]	-0.78 [-7.08]	-0.78 [-6.89]
	t-2	-0.44 [-3.4]	-0.56 [-4.18]	-0.56 [-4.07]
	t-3	-0.39 [-3.19]	-0.50 [-4.00]	-0.49 [-3.88]
	t-4	-0.25 [-2.37]	-0.33 [-3.1]	-0.32 [-2.97]
Δgdp	t-1	0.57 [2.07]	0.51 [1.91]	0.50 [1.84]
	t-2	0.19 [0.65]	0.19 [0.67]	0.16 [0.57]
	t-3	-0.02 [-0.06]	-0.05 [-0.20]	-0.06 [-0.23]
	t-4	0.11 [0.43]	0.11 [0.43]	0.10 [0.40]
Δp	t-1	-0.09 [-2.11]	-0.09 [-2.27]	-0.10 [-2.50]
	t-2	-0.07 [-1.61]	-0.08 [-1.92]	-0.09 [-2.09]
	t-3	-0.05 [-1.05]	-0.05 [-1.3]	-0.06 [-1.51]
	t-4	-0.08 [-1.71]	-0.10 [-2.23]	-0.10 [-2.29]
Δps	t-1	0.20 [2.21]	0.23 [2.65]	0.22 [2.51]
	t-2	-0.23 [-2.41]	-0.21 [-2.25]	-0.22 [-2.39]
	t-3	-0.09 [-0.86]	-0.08 [-0.81]	-0.08 [-0.87]
	t-4	-0.12 [-1.25]	-0.11 [-1.23]	-0.12 [-1.28]
Constant (γ_0)		0.01 [1.23]	0.02 [2.93]	0.02 [3.99]
Test statistics				
R^2		57%	61%	60%
Adjusted R^2		46%	51%	49%
Log likelihood		271.24	275.96	274.87
F-statistic		5.26	5.86	5.63

The values in parentheses are the t-values. According to Wald tests all lags are significant and all endogenous variables satisfy Granger causation tests. Other e-proxies do not improve the model compared with *eBank* and *eUse*. We prefer them because of better data quality.

The goodness of fit (R^2) of the three models is acceptable.[26] A graphical fit is shown in Section 2.5. In general, the coefficients have signs as expected and values that are in

---

[26] If the same model is estimated with data that was not seasonally adjusted, R^2 and adjusted R^2 are between 97% and 99% when seasonal dummies are included. The large difference to the values given in Table 3 stems from the predictive power of the seasonal dummies. Without the

line with previous studies. The long-run price elasticity is highly significant and ranges between -0.22 and -0.27. This tells us that a 10% increase in price will reduce total traffic between 2.2 and 2.7% in the long run. However, the speed of adjustment α seems to be quite small and it is not clear, *a priori*, what the adjustment dynamics are.

Figure 5 depicts the effect of a hypothetical 10% price increase at the beginning of year 2000 according to substitution model 1. The loss in volume converges to the prediction of the long-run price elasticity (as shown by the dotted line) after about three years. One would expect demand to be more price sensitive.[27]

Figure 5: Demand shock after a 10% price increase

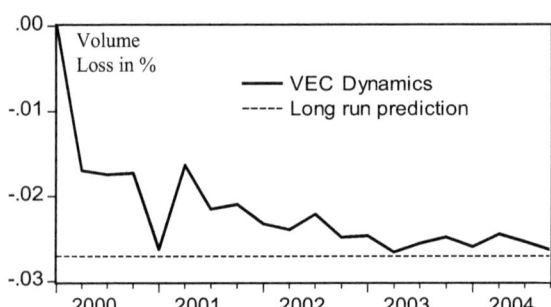

The main coefficient difference between the models is the long run elasticity of the substitutes' price *PS*; whereas the short run impact of a change in the *PS* is about the same among the three models, the long run effect is significant only in the traditional model. At the same time, the two e-proxies in the substitution models are highly significant. It appears that once *eBank* and *eUse* are included in the model, they provide a better approximation than the substitutes' price index does. An interpretation may be that the choice between writing a letter and sending an e-mail or SMS is dominated by other product properties than price.

---

seasonal adjustment, most of the variation in mail demand is caused by seasonality, which is well explained by quarterly dummies. To illustrate, a static regression for Q with only a constant, a trend, and quarterly dummies yields an adjusted R^2 of 84%.

[27] See Cazals et al. (2002) for a theoretical treatment, of why time series models exhibit often lower elasticities than cross-section models.

2.5 Forecasting future mail demand

How do the three models predict future mail demand? One general possibility for forecasting with a time series model is to solve the previously estimated static model with one's own or a third party's expectations about future realizations of the independent variables for every t in the forecasting horizon $t+1...T$. This approach leads to two kinds of forecasting error: (1) erroneous expectations, e.g., the assumption of future GDP growth proves to be under- or overestimated; and (2) specification error of the previously estimated model. A second general possibility for time-series forecasting is to estimate a dynamic model in lags, so no expectations about future values of explanatory variables are necessary, at least for the one-step-ahead forecast at $t+1$. Either way, the forecasting interval for a given confidence level increases with the length of the forecasting horizon.

In order to predict with our vector error correction model we need to mix the two ways to some extent. Note that equation (2) does not include any values of the endogenous variables at time t. Thus, for predicting mail demand for the next period $t+1$, the model does not build on GDP_{t+1}: it only uses GDP_t. This property is useful for performing one-step-ahead forecasts because the model needs observed values of the endogenous variables only. Even multi-step-ahead forecasts are possible without making any forecast of the explanatory variables. To explain this, we return to equation (2). The complete VEC specification includes analogous equations for the other endogenous variables GDP, P, and PS. Thus, to perform a forecast for time $t+2$, we can use the predicted endogenous values from $t+1$. However, we still need to make our own expectations of the two exogenous e-proxies.

Both kinds of forecasts were carried out. The first kind is done by treating all endogenous variables, other than total traffic, as exogenous[28]. Thus, we need to predict all the explanatory variables manually. For nominal GDP, we assume 1.8% growth per year. Further, we assume nominal price stability of postal prices, and we extrapolate CPI, PS, eBank and eUse according to their past trends.[29] We solve the model stochastically to obtain confidence bounds. The results for the forecasting period from 1990Q1 to 2007Q4 are shown in Figure 6, Figure 7, and Figure 8 on the left-hand side. The dotted line is the one-step confidence bound. From 1990Q1 to 2004Q4, the predicted values represent the model fit during the estimation period. The observations from 2005Q1 to 2007Q4 show the forecasts for the out-of-sample period. Observation 2005Q1 deserves special attention.

---

[28] This means that ΔQ_{t+2} is computed with our own expectation of GDP_{t+1} instead of the VEC prediction $\hat{GDP}_{t+1}$.

[29] Taken all together, this is quite a large set of assumptions.

It is the most recent realization of total traffic and enables an indicative reality check of the estimated models.

The right-hand side of Figure 6, Figure 7, and Figure 8 show the results from the endogenous stochastic solution of the model, i.e., only *eBank* and *eUse* are determined outside the model. The forecasting period starts in 2005Q1. The dotted lines represent the multi-step confidence bounds. Note that the solution does not account for coefficient uncertainty in linked equations.

The traditional model (TM) gives by far the most optimistic scenario for future mail demand. According to the model's results shown in Figure 6, mail demand has now entered a period of low but positive growth. The second graph (i.e. endogenous predictions) reveals that the model fit for the realization 2005Q1 is not as good as those obtained from the substitution models. On the other hand, the predictions for the other endogenous variables are by far the most realistic ones (not shown here).

Figure 6: Exogenous (left) and endogenous (right) predictions TM

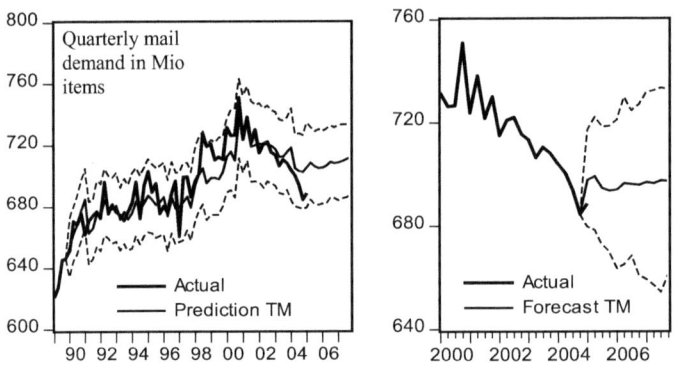

The most pessimistic outlook is given by substitution model 1 (SM1). According to the model, the decline in aggregate mail demand will continue at an accelerated speed (Figure 7). The one-step-ahead forecast for 2005Q4 is quite accurate. However, the predicted dynamics for the other exogenous variables are quite unrealistic. According to the endogenous solution, Switzerland will enter a heavy recession soon.

Figure 7: Exogenous (left) and endogenous (right) predictions SM1

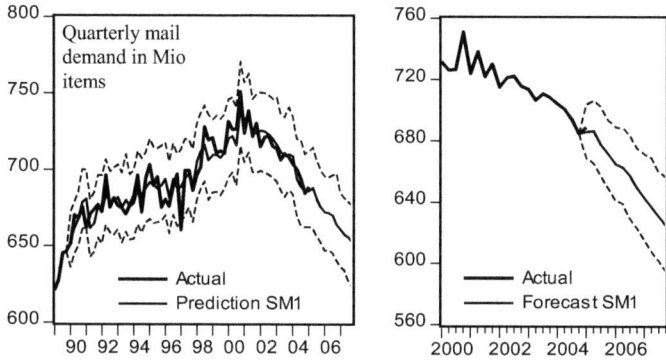

Substitution model 2 (SM2) lies somewhere in between the other two. The exogenous solution states that the decline is slowing down (Figure 8). The fit at 2005Q1 is almost perfect. In the endogenous model, the forecasts for GDP are again very pessimistic. This can be seen indirectly by comparing the two graphs; the decline is more severe in the endogenous calculations, because the (endogenous) forecast for GDP is much lower than our expectation of 1.8% growth.

Figure 8: Exogenous (left) and endogenous (right) predictions SM2

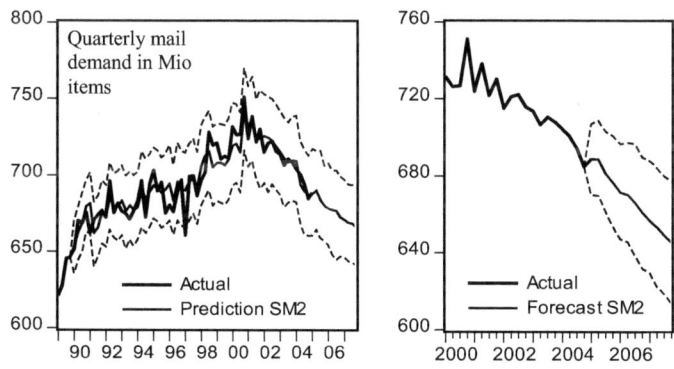

Comparing fit and forecast of the three models, each one has its own pros and cons. The traditional model exhibits the poorest fit, especially towards the end of the estimation period. As a direct consequence, the forecast performance at 2005Q1 is poor. Nevertheless, the endogenous predictions of GDP and prices seem to be the most realistic ones. Both substitution models predict an unrealistic negative development of future GDP. Still, they provide a better fit and a better one-step-ahead forecast.

2.6 Conclusions

E-substitution is one of the most crucial issues in the postal industry. Most postal services heavily depend on their core business of delivering physical mail – once the only form of advanced long distance communication. The primary threat of e-substitution lies in the historical business model of most postal services. Over time, larger mail volumes increased economies of scale[30] and enabled the postal services to keep postal rates low despite increasing labor costs and better service provision[31]. A comparison between the development of real wages and real postal rates illustrates the historical postal business model. Whereas real wages grew exponentially, Swiss Post's real rates are today even lower than in the 1920s. In short, e-substitution questions the stability of this business model. Moreover, the 'political universal service model' builds on growth of mail demand. The remarkable growth over the past 100 years enabled politicians to impose uniform rates and demanding service obligations on the postal services, i.e., nationwide coverage of home delivery, without undermining the financial viability of the postal service. However, e-substitution also brings into question the stability of the political universal service model.

The intent of our research was to forecast future mail volumes and thereby to assess future e-substitution. We estimated three vector error correction models with quarterly data of Swiss aggregate mail demand. We found strong evidence that e-substitution has happened in the past few years. Moreover, two of the three models indicate that e-substitution will continue to undermine mail demand in the short and medium term. For the long term, we dare no prediction; we conclude that it is nearly impossible to make long-run forecasts with the applied techniques, because there is no unique proxy for e-substitution. Every such proxy yields another result, and combining or merging different proxies brings the same set of problems (or makes it even impossible to find a cointegrated long-run relationship). In addition, we do not know what kind of new substitutes will emerge in the near future and whether these substitutes are represented in our current proxies.[32]

---

[30] For economics on the cost structure of postal services see among others NERA (2004). For a detailed discussion on economies of scale and density in mail delivery see Chapter 3.

[31] Over time, most postal services significantly increased their services, e.g. P.O. box delivery was complemented with home delivery. An interesting case on the development of Universal Service in the United States provides Campbell (2004).

[32] Cross-sectional econometric methods such as discrete choice analysis could resolve the problem. Nonetheless, we believe that the design of a survey with choices over hypothetical e-products would cause similar problems as e-proxies do here.

Despite these limitations for long forecasting horizons, the short-run predictions seem to be accurate. Here we see the strengths of vector error correction models. They are powerful tools for forecasting the near future because they combine explanatory variables in levels, differences, and lags and still provide an economic interpretation of the results.

Inevitably, we do not know how severely e-substitution will affect mail volumes in the future. However, our model predictions are not optimistic, ranging from accelerated decline to slow growth. We therefore recommend for politicians and regulators to find universal service policies that do not increase the universal service provider's fixed costs.

A key issue going forward for postal services will be not to rely solely on their historical business models and to prepare for the worst. In fact, many operators have initiated projects to respond to this uncertainty, e.g. with diversification into new product lines and with programs to make costs more responsive to (potentially declining) demand conditions (i.e. reduce fraction of fixed costs).

Figure 9: E-Substitution as a loss of market share in platform competition

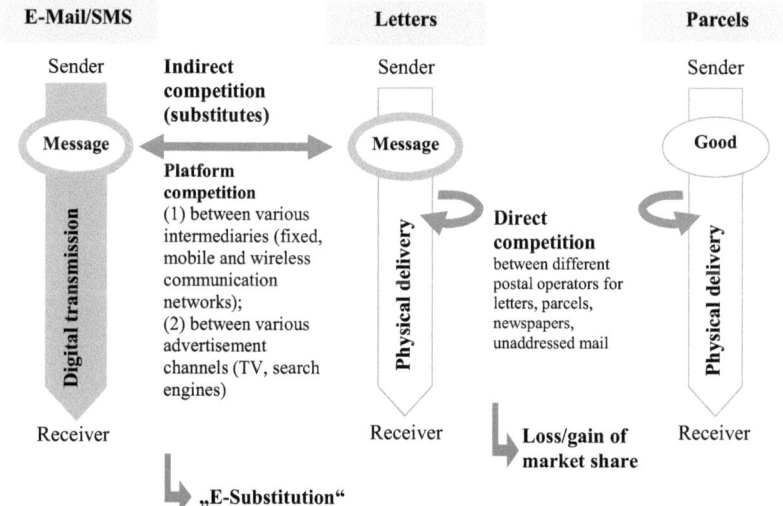

In the same time, it is important to understand e-substitution as a result of competition of letters against other platforms of communications (transactional mail/direct mail against E-Mail, SMS, internet platforms, etc), and other means for advertising (direct mail against TV, newspapers, etc). Figure 9 illustrates this "indirect competition" or "platform competition" in contrast to "direct competition", where postal operators directly compete against themselves for the delivery of physical letters. Hence, it is crucial that postal services understand e-substitution not just as an inevitable matter of fact, but as a competitive outcome of platform competition, where yet the "battle for mail" is not lost[33]. In this light, postal services increasingly are starting to position mail within the broader communications, internet and advertising industry[34].

---

[33] Figure 4 illustrates this evolving and increasing "indirect" competition: Price elasticities increased over time (i.e. more negative), most probably because of emerging substitutes, whereas cross-price elasticities got statistically significant, most probably because the telecommunications index increasingly included prices of new substitutes such as SMS and access to the internet (E-Mail).

[34] Examples include USPS' and Pitney Bowes' campaigns for mail in the US.

3. Economies of Scale, Density and Scope in Mail Delivery

3.1 Introduction

In the letters market, the postal value chain can be segmented into the four main processes collection, sorting, transportation, and delivery as depicted in Figure 10. Collection takes many forms. The traditional retail channels are post offices, postal partners[35], and mail drop boxes. Large customers additionally have the possibility to use customized business counters (e.g. located at sorting centers), direct collection by postal operators, or electronic delivery of data to specialized letter shops. Sorting is in most countries done in two steps. Outbound-sorting involves a first run, where the mail is sorted to the first two or three digits of the postal zip code, and inbound-sorting typically involves the final sorting on carrier route level. Delivery is done mainly by mail carriers who first sequence the mail ("walk sorting") before physically delivering the mail of their routes to mail boxes. It is important to note that delivery accounts for the largest fraction of total cost of postal end-to-end operators.

Figure 10: The postal value chain

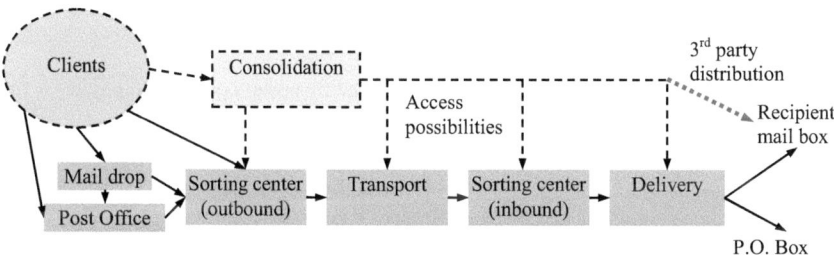

Table 4 depicts that delivery of physical mail accounts for about 50 percent of total costs of postal operators. Hence, inefficiencies in mail delivery are of particular importance and face increasing management attention. New econometric approaches have the potential to serve decision makers in several crucial issues: implementing internal benchmarking tools to promote internal competition between decision units, to determine

---

[35] E.g. grocery stores offering basic postal services. Main examples are the liberalized postal markets of Sweden and New Zealand. For a discussion of the regulatory model of these two countries in reference to Switzerland see Jaag and Trinkner (2007).

the optimal size of delivery units, to assess where mail and parcels services should be provided by joint or separate delivery units, and to know how much costs are dependent on volumes.

Table 4: Distribution of total costs

	Overhead	Collection	Sorting	Transport	Delivery
Letters	16%	12%	15%	7%	50%
Parcels	13%	10%	17%	21%	39%

Source: NERA (2004)

The empirical part of the chapter assesses the three latter issues using an econometric approach. We analyze the cost structure of a sample of mail delivery units from Swiss Post. In 2004, Swiss Post organized these units in four regions. In every region, various mail delivery centers lead a small number of local delivery units. These delivery units are the main starting point for a total of 10,000 mail carriers that deliver letters six times a week to almost every household in Switzerland.

We estimate a quadratic cost function employing a cross-section data set from Swiss Post from 2004 with information on 327 postal units, most of them delivering parcels as well. The quadratic specification enables us to estimate measures of economies of scale and density as well as economies of scope between mail and parcels.

The empirical results of this study could be used by postal operators in particular for strategic planning, to decide whether letters and parcels should be delivered joint or separate, and to define the optimal size of the service area for each delivery unit. The results are further useful for policy makers to assess the impact of the letter market liberalization on the industry's cost structure.

The chapter is organized as follows and id based to a large extent on Farsi, Filippini and Trinkner (2006). Section 3.2 outlines the main contribution of our research relative to the most important papers in the field. Section 3.3 presents the model specifications. Section 3.4 introduces the data, and Section 3.5 provides the estimation results. We compute the measures for economies of scale, density and scope in Section 3.6 and conclude in Section 3.7. We find empirical evidence for economies of scale, density, and scope. Section 3.8 discusses some important corollaries in the context of the theory of contestable markets and natural monopolies.

3.2 Background

In the literature, there are few published studies on the economies of scale and scope of postal services.[36] The most recent studies relevant for our study are those by Wada, et. al. (1997), Gazzei et al. (2002), Mizutani and Uranishi (2003), Cazals et al. (2005) and Filippini and Zola (2005).

Wada, Tsunoda and Nemoto (1997) estimate a multiproduct total cost function of the Japanese mail service by treating the delivery of letter mail and that of parcels as two independent outputs. In their study, they consider panel data covering 12 regional postal offices collected over a 15-year period from 1980 to 1994. Using a translog cost function they find evidence for the existence of overall economies of scale. Furthermore, the estimation of a generalized translog function highlights significant product-specific economies of scale for letter mail, but not for parcels.

Gazzei et al. (2002) apply a multiproduct cost function to analyze a database consisting of a cross-section of 9168 French post offices operating over the year 1999. The results of their empirical analysis, based on a log-log cost function, suggest the presence of economies of scale. In spite the fact that these authors estimate a multiproduct cost function, no estimation on the economies of scope is provided. The reason is that the log-log functional form does not allow the computation of the economies of scope.

Mizutani and Uranishi (2003) perform an econometric analysis of economies of scale using a single-output cost model, considering the public company (Post Office) and five other private carriers operating in Japan. Through the econometric estimation of a translog total cost function using a pooled data set over the period 1972-1998, they find no evidence for the hypothesis of the presence of economies of scale for this industry.

Cazals, Florens and Soteri (2005) assume a log-linear specification to analyze panel data of Royal Mail's delivery units. By estimating the cost elasticity for various sub-samples, they highlight the importance of the unobserved heterogeneity in the estimation of scale economies especially in the rural areas. They also point out that the economies of scale in delivery mainly originate from the key variable traffic per delivery point. The scope economies have not been estimated.

The paper by Filippini and Zola (2005) investigates scale and cost efficiency of a sample of Swiss postal offices. The paper considers estimation of a log-log multiproduct cost function employing a cross-section data set on small local post offices. The empirical evidence indicates the existence of economies of scale. Further, the outcome of this

---

[36] See NERA (2004) for an overview of the empirical literature in this field.

analysis shows that approximately 50% of the postal offices operate close to the regional standard for efficiency. Again, the authors do not provide empirical evidence on economies of scope because of the use of the log-log functional form.

Most of these studies have used a log-log or a translog functional form.[37] These functional forms have a drawback compared to other forms such as quadratic in that they do not provide a straightforward estimation method for economies of scope.[38]

The concept of scope economies (Baumol et al., 1982) can only be estimated if the cost function allows a zero value for outputs, which is not the case in any logarithmic form. There are few studies that have tried an estimation of scope economies in line with the classical definition. One exception is Wada et al. (1997), who have used a generalized translog form with Box-Cox transformation to overcome the problem of zero output. In this chapter we are interested to analyze both economies of scale and economies of scope. For this reason, we follow Baumol et al. (1982) and use a quadratic functional form in which the scope economies can be directly identified.

The three major differences of this study in comparison to the studies discussed before are (1) the utilization of a quadratic functional form, (2) the use of an econometric procedure that takes into account the heteroscedasticity problem typical for a sample that contains small as well very large production units, and (3) the estimation of a cost function for the delivery units of Swiss Post.

3.3 Model specification an econometric methods

The adopted model is based on a quadratic cost function with two outputs namely, mail (Y_1) and parcel (Y_2) and two input factors: labor and capital. The outputs are calculated as an adjusted sum of the number of letters (parcels) delivered. Letters, for which the postal carrier needs more time for delivery, are weighted more than ordinary letters. Labor price (P_L) is measured as the average annual salary of a full-time-equivalent employee engaged in delivery. Capital price (P_K) is measured as the ratio of the non-labor expenses to a measure of physical capital. This latter measure is taken is a weighted sum

---

[37] See for example Cazals et al. (2001), Mizutani and Uranishi (2003), Wada et al. (1997) and Gori et al. (2005).

[38] A major shortcoming of the translog functional form is that, since the natural logarithm of zero is not defined, it can only be used for multiproduct producers that supply positive quantities in all outputs. This problem can be solved by incorporating a Box-Cox transformation of the output variables. However, the translog functional form incorporating this transformation is non-linear in its parameters and therefore harder to estimate.

of the number of vehicles owned by the postal unit. This measure has its clear limitations, but is the only one available.

In addition to outputs and input prices, two output characteristics have been included: These variables include the number of delivery points in the service area (denoted by H) and the number of affiliated local delivery units (B), which is a positive value for the regional delivery centers that are usually linked to several local delivery units. It is set to zero for local units. In addition, three dummies (R_1, R_2, R_3) representing the north, east, west and southern regions are included.

The resulting specification of the cost function can be written as:

$$C = C(Y_1, Y_2, P_L, P_K, H, B, R_1, R_2, R_3) \qquad (3),$$

where C represents total cost and the explanatory variables are defined as above.

A quadratic functional form is used. As explained in the previous Section, this functional form provides a readily applicable expression for the economies of scope. Moreover, because of the presence of zero parcel output in some of the delivery units (about 12.5% of the sample) logarithmic forms like Cobb-Douglas and translog would require additional adjustments. The cost function can be written as:

$$\begin{aligned} C_i = {} & \beta_0 + \beta_1 Y_{1i} + \beta_2 Y_{2i} + \tfrac{\beta_{11}}{2}(Y_{1i})^2 + \tfrac{\beta_{22}}{2}(Y_{2i})^2 + \beta_{12} Y_{1i} Y_{2i} \\ & + \beta_K P_{Ki} + \beta_L P_{Li} + \beta_H H_i + \beta_B B_i + \delta_1 R_{1i} + \delta_2 R_{2i} + \delta_3 R_{3i} + \varepsilon_i \end{aligned} \qquad (4),$$

with $i = 1, 2, \ldots, N$, where subscript i denotes the delivery unit; N is the number of delivery units; and ε_i is the error term. All the explanatory variables are normalized, namely, they are replaced by their deviations from their respective median values. Four econometric specifications have been considered: The first model (Model I) is an Ordinary Least Squares (OLS) model in which the error term (ε_i) is assumed to be identically and independently distributed across the delivery units.

In the remaining models, the error term has a more general structure that allows for heteroscedasticity. Three cases have been considered: Model II is a Weighted Least Squares (WLS) in which variances are assumed to be proportional to the square of the mean of the dependent variable as predicted by the OLS model (denoted by C_i^{OLS}). Model III is also a WLS model but with variances proportional to the square of the total deliveries (Y) including mail and parcel outputs. Finally Model IV is a Multiplicative Heteroscedastic (MH) regression model in which the variance is assumed to be an exponential function of total deliveries (Y) and a binary indicator (D) distinguishing the delivery centers from the regional delivery units. The latter model has been estimated by the full-information maximum likelihood method, which requires the assumption of normality. The specification of variances in the adopted models can be summarized as:

$$\begin{aligned}
&\text{Model } I \text{ (OLS): } \varepsilon_i \sim iid(0,\sigma^2) \\
&\text{Model } II \text{ (WLS): } \varepsilon_i \sim iid(0,\sigma_i^2), \; \sigma_i^2 = \sigma^2 (C_i^{OLS})^2 \\
&\text{Model } III \text{ (WLS): } \varepsilon_i \sim iid(0,\sigma_i^2), \; \sigma_i^2 = \sigma^2 (Y_i)^2 \\
&\text{Model } IV \text{ (MH): } \varepsilon_i \sim N(0,\sigma_i^2), \; \sigma_i^2 = \sigma^2 \exp(\gamma_1 Y_i + \gamma_2 D_i)
\end{aligned} \quad (5).$$

3.4 Data

The data consist of a cross section of 328 mail delivery units operated by Swiss Post's letter section. These units are organized as 241 local delivery units and 87 regional centers. The operation of each local unit is monitored by the corresponding regional delivery center which in turn is attached to one of four delivery zones (cf. Figure 11). All the regional centers have also local delivery tasks. The number of delivery units attached to a regional delivery center varies considerably and averages about three units per center. The final regression sample consists of 327 observations including 86 regional centers[39] and 241 local delivery units. The various units cover a wide range of output and costs, varying from 1.3 to over 50 million deliveries.

Figure 11: Swiss Post's organization of mail delivery as of 2004

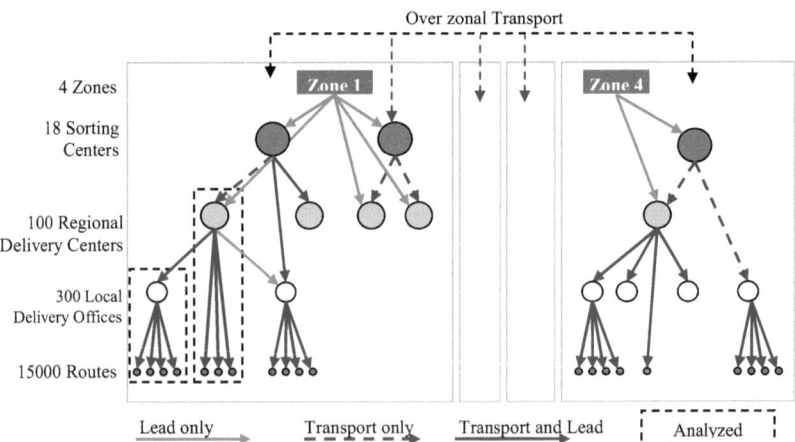

---

[39] We had to exclude one of the regional delivery centers from the sample because of missing values for costs.

Most of the studied mail delivery units also provide parcels deliveries in rural areas. In about 16 percent of the delivery units the number of delivered parcels is very small (less than 100 for the entire one-year period). The number of delivery points varies quite considerably across the delivery units.

As the operation of delivery centers includes the additional responsibility of monitoring the local units within their regional zone, one could argue that these centers should be analyzed separately. However, our preliminary regressions using the OLS specification in (4), and with the appropriate interaction terms indicated that the differences between the coefficients across local units and regional centers are not statistically significant. Therefore, we consider both categories in a single sample. It should be noted that although the regional centers are on average significantly larger than the local units, this is not a general rule. The t-tests show that while both mail output and number of delivery points are on average significantly larger in regional offices, the parcel output volume is not significantly different across the two categories.

3.5 Estimation results

The models explained in Equations (4) and (5) have been estimated for the sample. The regression results are listed in Farsi et al. (2006). The first observation is that most of the explanatory variables show statistically significant effects with the expected signs. An exception is the input factor prices. The coefficients of both labor and capital prices are insignificant, suggesting that cost differences across companies are not driven by differences in input prices.[40]

Secondly, the results of Model I that does not consider the heteroscedasticity are significantly different from the other three models. In particular, according to this model, the parcel output does not have a significant effect on costs (at 5% significance level), whereas unlike other models, the output interaction term (Y_1Y_2) has a positive and significant effect on costs. These differences suggest that ignoring heteroscedasticity might cause misleading results not only regarding standard errors and significance but for the coefficients as well. Another interesting observation is that all region dummies are highly significant suggesting that postal networks in different areas depend on certain unobserved region-specific characteristics.

---

[40] This result could be related to the measurement errors incurred in the estimation of prices. However, it is not surprising as we consider decision units from the same company.

Among the models, starting from OLS model that does not account for heteroscedasticity, there is a specific order across the remaining three models. Model *II* accounts for heteroscedasticity through the existing variables in the mode. Model *III* goes one step further in that the variations are adjusted using an additional variable (total deliveries). Finally, Model *IV* defines a structure for heteroscedasticity based on two additional variables (total deliveries and regional unit dummy). As the results listed in Farsi et al. (2006) indicate, the pattern of variation of the estimated coefficients across different models confirms the existence of heteroscedasticity bias. We contend that Model *IV* results should be considered as the best estimates among the presented models. According to this model, the output coefficient of mail is on average about 0.19. Each customer (delivery point) has a marginal cost of CHF 70 and each additional branch has a cost burden of about CHF 100,000 for a regional unit.

3.6 Economies of scale, density and scope

The inclusion in the cost function (5) of the number of delivery points allows for the distinction of economies of scale (*ES*), economies of density (*ED*), and economies of scope (*ESS*).

In a multiproduct setting, *economies of scale* are defined as those reductions in ray average cost when all outputs and number of delivery points are increased proportionally, holding all input prices fixed. E.g., merging two local units would save money when *ES* are positive. *Economies of density* exist if simultaneously increasing the production of all outputs, holding the number of delivery points fixed, lowers ray average cost. Thus, positive *ED* would mean that Swiss Post's unit costs would increase in case mail demand where to be shrinking (e.g. because of E-Substitution or shrinking market shares). *Economies of scope* are present when there are cost efficiencies to be gained by joint production of multiple outputs. If *ESS* between mail and parcels are locally present, it makes sense to provide the two services with the same carrier.

Following Baumol et al. (1982) economies of scale, density and scope in a multi-output setting are respectively defined as:

$$ES \equiv \frac{C}{Y_1 \frac{\partial C}{\partial Y_1} + Y_2 \frac{\partial C}{\partial Y_2} + H \frac{\partial C}{\partial H}} = \frac{C}{\beta_1 Y_1 + \beta_2 Y_2 + \beta_{11}(Y_1)^2 + \beta_{22}(Y_2)^2 + 2\beta_{12}Y_1Y_2 + \beta_H H}$$

$$ED \equiv \frac{C}{Y_1 \frac{\partial C}{\partial Y_1} + Y_2 \frac{\partial C}{\partial Y_2}} = \frac{C}{\beta_1 Y_1 + \beta_2 Y_2 + \beta_{11}(Y_1)^2 + \beta_{22}(Y_2)^2 + 2\beta_{12}Y_1Y_2} \quad (6).$$

$$ESS \equiv \frac{C(Y_1,0) + C(0,Y_2) - C(Y_1,Y_2)}{C(Y_1,Y_2)}$$

The estimated values of economies of scale, density and scope are given in Table 5. These values have been estimated based on equations (6) for each one of the delivery units in the sample. Taking into account the experiences from other countries, the levels of the variables should be treated with caution because of the lack of panel data. However, the relative altitudes are important. The results indicate that virtually in all companies and across all models, the scope economies are positive. Similarly, the constant of density economies is higher than 1 in almost all companies suggesting the existence of density economies in a large majority of the cases.[41] The constants of scale economies are also higher than 1 in a small majority of the observations. However, in about 20 to 25 percent of the cases, this constant is either less than 1 or very close to 1, suggesting that scale economies are not considerable in many cases.

Table 5: Economies of scope, scale and density

	Model I	Model II	Model III	Model IV
Scale economies:				
1st quantile	0.389	0.346	0.305	0.341
Median	0.455	0.378	0.334	0.372
3rd quantile	0.519	0.417	0.377	0.410
Correlation with Y	NS	-0.173	NS	-0.374
Density economies:				
1st quantile	1.033	1.084	1.057	1.036
Median	1.109	1.147	1.102	1.112
3rd quantile	1.207	1.216	1.162	1.187
Correlation with Y	-0.267	-0.463	-0.387	-0.575
Scope economies:				
1st quantile	1.594	1.477	1.401	1.390
Median	1.794	1.542	1.457	1.477
3rd quantile	2.021	1.645	1.556	1.587
Correlation with Y	-0.164	-0.389	-0.264	-0.570

NS = not significant;
Model I: OLS; Model II: WLS with weights being the OLS prediction; Model III: WLS with weights being the total deliveries; Model IV: Multiplicative heteroscendastic regression.

The results suggest that scope economies are considerable across mail and parcel services especially in regions with low mail and parcels volume (negative correlation with Y). This supports Swiss Post's policy to combine the two services in rural areas. According to Model *IV*, combining parcel and mail can save a considerable amount of the total costs compared to a case, in which two delivery units operate mail and parcel

---

[41] There is only one unit that according to the OLS model, has negative scope economies and diseconomies of density and scope. Model *IV* predicts diseconomies of density only for 5 units.

separately. The estimated density economies suggest that an increase of mail demand, that goes not together with increasing the number of delivery points (extending network) reduces average costs per piece of mail and vice versa. On the other hand, the estimated scale economies suggest that in many cases, if such an increase involves an extension in the network or an increase in the number of customers, the economies will not be considerable. However, the results suggest that at least about half of the units included in the sample do not fully exploit the potential scale economies. The significant negative correlation with the output suggests that the scale economies are lower for large delivery units. In other words, the figures indicate that there is some potential for Swiss Post in merging some of the smaller delivery units. However, geographical reasons may restrict the potential of such a merger program.

3.7 Conclusions

The purpose of this study was to analyze the cost structure of Swiss Post's delivery units in order to assess economies of scale, economies of density and economies of scope. In particular, policy-makers are interested in cost information of this industry in order to determine the desirability of competition in the postal delivery sector. Moreover, from a company point of view, the management of Swiss Post can be interested in having some information on the economies of scale and scope in order to define a policy on combining individual operating units.

A quadratic total cost function was estimated using a cross section of 327 delivery units for the year 2004. The empirical results indicate the existence of economies of density, economies of scale and economies of scope especially for units with low mail volumes.

The results on economies of scale suggest that a considerable portion of the postal delivery units seem to operate at an inappropriately low scale. The service territory area of most of these units appear too small to produce at optimal scale. Therefore, if geographically feasible, mergers between two small units whose service territories are adjacent would improve the scale efficiency of these units.

The estimated economies of density can help to clarify the efficiency of side-by-side ("end-to-end") competition at all points of a given service territory versus monopolistic provision of delivery postal services. The finding shows that the cost of serving a market of size y over a municipal territory with one delivery unit is lower than the cost of serving the same market with n competitive delivery units that install parallel facilities everywhere. Therefore, side-by-side competition is less cost-efficient than the monopolistic distribution of postal services. Our findings offer some support to the policy of monopoly-based postal delivery regulations such as the US model "worksharing" (for details the reader is referred to Section 4). In the US, a mandatory access-regime is in place, where access to the incumbent's network is not only possible, but also mandatory: It is not allowed to bypass the delivery network of the incumbent USPS. It is important to point out that such a system is not possible once end-to-end competition is introduced as it is the case in the UK. These results are in line with various market entry models. Section 4 provides more background and an overall welfare assessment of various liberalization policies.

The presence of economies of scope shows that an unbundling of a multi-output company into single-output companies leads to higher costs in the market as the synergies in the joint (rural) production are no more exploited. This implies that the two postal delivery services, mail and parcels should be provided by the same delivery unit at least in rural areas. Again, the US system is economically supported: The USPS offers access for parcels. This product is utilized mainly for parcels destined to rural areas.

3.8 Discussion: Mail delivery as a *contested* natural monopoly

In Section 3.6 we have estimated economies of scale and scope simultaneously. This enables us to draw some conclusions on the question whether delivery of mail satisfies the properties of a natural monopoly or not.

An industry is said to have the property of a natural monopoly if one single firm can produce a given output at a lower cost than two or more firms. More precisely, we can speak of a natural monopoly if the cost function for producing a set of outputs is subadditive in the relevant range of output vectors. This condition implies that the costs of producing a vector of outputs as a whole are less than the costs of producing the same output subdivided in any combination of subsets. For a precise definition the reader is referred to Baumol (1977).

In the single-output case, cost function $C(y)$ is subadditive for output y if the production of any output combination $y_1, \ldots, y_m$ satisfying $\sum_{i=1}^{m} y_i = y$ (with at least two $y_i \neq 0$) is more costly than integrated production:

$$C(y) < \sum_{i=1}^{m} C(y_i).$$

To illustrate, if it was not possible to distribute letters together with any other items such as parcels (that is we are in the single-product case), the presence of economies of scale and density would imply decreasing average costs and hence subadditivity.

However, letters are most often distributed together with parcels, unaddressed mail, value added services such as registered mail, and others. Baumol (1977) shows that in such a multi-product case economies of scale and density are nor a necessary nor a sufficient condition. The underlying reasons are economies or diseconomies of scope between the various products. Thereby, economies of scope are a necessary, but not sufficient condition for subadditivity in the multi-product case. As Baumol, Panzar and Willig (1982) point out, even the presence of both economies of scale and scope (as our estimations indicate) are not sufficient – for example two products might exhibit moderate economies scale and scope in joint production, but each individually very high economies of scale. Hence, the subadditivity property implies that a global test for any combination of outputs should be conducted.

In the postal sector there have been some econometric attempts to shed light on the natural monopoly property of letter delivery. Bradley and Colvin (1995) and Wada et al. (1997) find mixed evidence on cost subadditivity depending on the cost function specification in the provision of letter and parcel services. Although we did not apply a global test for subadditivity, the simultaneous presence of economies of scale and scope (cf. Table 5) together with limited economies of scale in BtoC parcels delivery[42] points towards a natural monopoly. Similarly, most economists regard letters delivery as a (contestable) natural monopoly. Cremer (2000, p. 49) states that "there seems to be a widespread consensus that at least one segment of the network, namely distribution is a natural monopoly".

However, even if mail delivery is a natural monopoly, it is important to note that it is to be considered a *contestable* natural monopoly. Contestability refers to the contestable markets theory that goes back on Baumol, Panzar and Willig (1982) and essentially expands economic efficiency properties based on the assumption of perfect markets to industries exhibiting subadditive cost structures *provided there are no relevant sunk costs*. In such markets operators do not succeed in preventing entry unless prices are set according to marginal costs. If in contrast sunk costs are present, we speak of a "monopolistic bottleneck" (see Table 6) which would raise the issue of stable market power with a respective justification for access regulation.

---

[42] In BtoC parcels delivery, where delivery points are varying day by day, the fraction of fixed costs is much smaller than in BtoC letters delivery, where mail carriers face fixed routes times in countries with high mail volumes per capita such as Switzerland.

Given the cost characteristics of mail delivery, no relevant sunk costs can be identified. Panzar (2002a) for example states that "there is little need to make such large sunk investments in the provision of postal and delivery services, since the bulk of postal costs are labor costs" and concludes in Panzar (2002b) that "postal markets are readily *contested*". Among others, Knieps (2002), seco (2005), Vaterlaus et al. (2003, 2007) argue that there are no monopolistic bottlenecks in the letters market.

Table 6: Contestability in dependence of cost characteristics

Network area	With sunk costs	Without sunk costs
Natural monopoly	Monopolistic bottlenecks	Potential competition (Contestable Networks)
No natural monopoly	Competition among active providers	Competition among active providers

Source: Knieps (2005)

Note that the concept of potential competition predicts no market entries for the mail market. Yet in practice we observe new entrants in deregulated postal markets such as New Zealand or Sweden[43]. Thus, either the theory of contestable markets fails, or postal markets are not to be classified as natural monopolies, or some other reasons enable new entrants more competitive cost structures with successful market entries. One important element that determines the cost structure of postal incumbents is the universal service obligation (USO). This constraint is imposed either on the market (i.e. public procurement, pay or play rules) or to the historical operator (asymmetric designation) with the latter being the only solution applied in practice so far[44].

Thereby, one USO constraint in particular limits the full exploitation of economies of scale, density and scope as computed above: The requirement to distribute *every working day* significantly reduces the universal service providers (USP) possibility to exploit economies of density compared to new entrants who limit their delivery to once or twice per week only. For example, Swiss Post is by law obliged not to fully exploit economies of density (at least 5 deliveries per week) which gives leeway for new entrants to enter the market for slow mail. Real world examples include Sandd from the Netherlands and CityMail from Sweden which both deliver twice a week. Moreover, recapitulate from our estimations that economies of scale are limited for large units, i.e. entrants can reach *better* economies of scale than incumbents by distributing in selected

---

[43] Cf. Andersson (2006) for an overview.
[44] Germany foresees a public procurement procedure after complete liberalization. FMO is scheduled for 2008. Debates on prolonging Deutsche Post's exclusive license are ongoing.

geographic areas only (as for example CityMail in Sweden which limits its delivery areas to densely populated regions).

We conclude that the postal distribution constitutes not only a contestable natural monopoly. It is a readily *contested natural monopoly* whose *economies of density are not completely exploited because of USO constraints*. In light of various market entries observed in (partially) liberalized markets, this interpretation offers a reasonable explanation for our simulation results as presented in Section 4.[45]

In terms of overall economic welfare these findings raise some important questions. Market entries that build on incumbent USO constraints (one might think of picking the cherries grown by USO constraints) and raise the incumbent's per piece costs and therefore are not necessary socially or economically efficient. For the overall welfare consequences the reader is referred to Section 4. However, the USO issue further limits the potential of end-to-end competition and potentially favors market models based on restricted entry in delivery (reserved areas or worksharing) where economies of density are optimally exploited given USO constraints.

---

[45] Besides asymmetric USO constraints other possible explanations include inefficiencies of postal operators, strategic decisions of mailers (e.g. press titles), or stranded costs such as higher salaries due to the civil servant status of the past. According to Cohen et al. (1997), Swiss Posts advantage due to scale effects is smaller than its disadvantage due to higher labor costs.

4. Overall Welfare Impact of Various Scenarios of Liberalization

4.1 Introduction

The European Union is about to open up its domestic letter markets for end-to-end competition by gradually abolishing the reserved areas of the former historical state-owned incumbents. According to Directive 2008/6/EC, the last postal monopoly in the EC will be history in 2013[46]. In contrast to the European developments, the United States developed worksharing as a means to introduce competition in the postal sector. Worksharing is an access like outsourcing policy based on a rigid letters monopoly where private operations are compensated for upstream activities by USPS's avoided costs. Up to now, the only example of a combination of the two policies is Great Britain. This combination is referred to as "access with bypass". However, worldwide letter services remain national monopolies in most countries. Figure 12 provides an overview of the four main regulations of letters markets.

As introduced in Chapter 1, the Swiss universal service provider (USP) is Swiss Post, which currently enjoys a (residual) monopoly on addressed letters up to a weight of 100 grams. The Swiss government has the power to open up the letter market *if the provision of the universal service obligation (USO) remains guaranteed*. Hence, prior to any further market opening, it is crucial to know how competition affects the financial viability of Swiss Post with or without a licensing system. Such a licensing system has been introduced in the liberalized parcels market. The Swiss regulatory authority PostReg is entitled to collect licensing fees that amount up to 3% on an entrant's turnover to compensate Swiss Post for its universal service provision if needed. Up to now, licensees have not been charged anything as Swiss Post's obligations have been outweighed by the residual monopoly.

The chapter provides insights on the consequences of different kinds of liberalization and regulation of the Swiss letter market. In contrast to PWC (2006b) we examine welfare effects and financial consequences for both Swiss Post and potential

---

[46] A short overview on the debate in Europe provides Finger (2007). Cf. Trinkner (2008) for a discussion of the 2008 postal directive. Note that, despite full market opening, most European countries will continue to grant their historical operators VAT exemptions on universal services. Examples include the UK, Germany and France. Given VAT rates of about 20%, such policies might result in market entry barriers and continuing de facto monopolies.

market entrants. We start with an analysis of what would happen if the current regulation of the parcels market were applied to the letter market.

Figure 12: Overview over various liberalization and regulatory policies

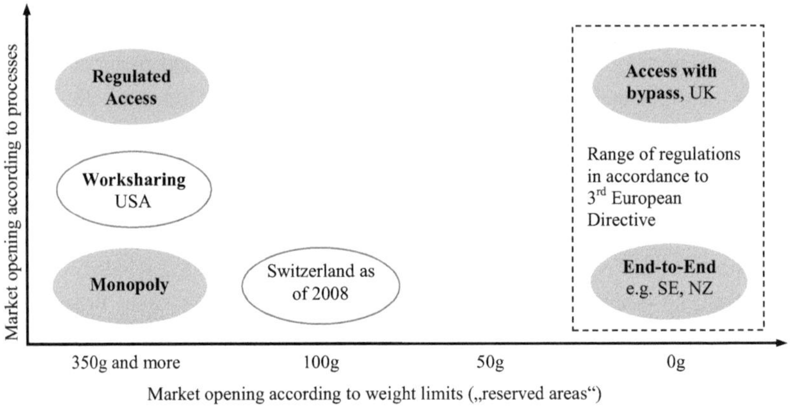

	350g and more	100g	50g	0g
	Regulated Access			Access with bypass, UK
	Worksharing USA			Range of regulations in accordance to 3rd European Directive
	Monopoly	Switzerland as of 2008		End-to-End e.g. SE, NZ

Market opening according to processes (vertical axis)
Market opening according to weight limits ("reserved areas") (horizontal axis)

The chapter proceeds as follows and bases on Dietl, Trinkner and Bleisch (2005). In Section 4.2, we develop and tailor a game theoretic model to the Swiss postal system. In Section 4.3, we calibrate the model with Swiss data. Section 4.4 presents our results on end-to-end competition and compares them with an evaluation of the regulated monopoly of 2003. We show that end-to-end competition results in lower welfare and problems to finance the USO even if a licensing system is introduced. Building on these results, we expand the model in Section 4.5 and analyze alternative regulatory scenarios. We show that worksharing will increase economic welfare. Section 4.7 contains a discussion and our main conclusions.

4.2 Basic model and formal results

The main challenge in assessing consequences of various liberalization and regulation scenarios to the Swiss letter market is to correctly predict future outcomes of competition. We know the figures of the (residual) monopoly regulation of today, but we do not know how new entrants will enter the market and how the various market players will behave. Economists all agree that for the case of "perfect competition", liberalization would increase overall welfare due to better products at lower costs (marginal cost rule). However, in reality, perfect markets do not exist. Hence, we have to systematically relax some key assumptions of perfect markets in order to develop a market model that maps reality in a stylized and reasonable way.

4.2.1. Modeling competition in postal markets

The experience of liberalized network industries including posts indicates that we have to expect oligopolistic competition with just view market players. I.e., *strategic interaction* takes place between operators and prices are rarely set according to marginal costs. Most probably, game theory has to be applied, especially if the industry's cost structure does not exhibit constant returns to scale as shown in Chapter 3. Completely liberalized letters markets such as Sweden, Finland, the UK, or New Zealand point into the same direction. Further, we have to deal with the issue of *"universal service"*, which is imposed on the market by regulations in different variations. For example, if the universal service obligation (USO) was imposed on just one market player (just duties, no rights), this could distort the competitive outcome and could harm the viability of the universal service provider (USP).

Thus, the effects of competition on prices, quality, innovation, overall welfare, and universal service provision and financing are not a priori clear. In order to analyze the effects of liberalization in the Swiss letter market, we use a standard game theoretic approach as outlined in Figure 13. We use a Bertrand competition framework with product differentiation to reflect that there are no binding capacity constraints in the postal sector. Furthermore, we observe large price spreads in liberalized market segments combined with some differentiation of operators in terms of product features and quality.

On the supply side, we let Swiss Post as incumbent I compete with a representative entrant E. The demand side links the two operators. Customers value the available products with respect to quality and prices. Strategic interaction takes place, where one operator's behavior affects both operators' profits. For example, when the incumbent raises its prices, some consumers will switch to the entrant and boost the entrant's sales. Further, a licensing system is introduced, where entrants eventually have to pay licensing fees in order to compensate the incumbent for its USO-obligations. By identifying Nash solutions, we can compute equilibrium prices which determine quantities, profits and overall welfare.

Figure 13: Model outline

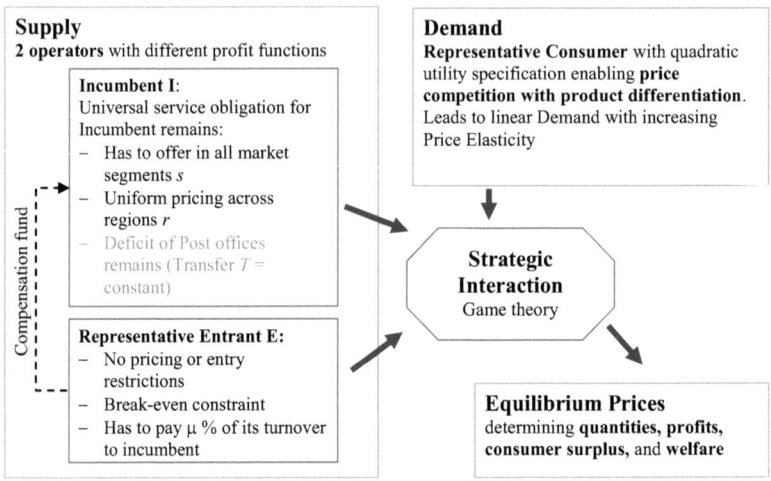

Technically speaking we use a Dixit-like approach to model price competition with product differentiation and assume that there are no information asymmetries.

4.2.2. Model specification

On the *demand side*, we assume a representative sender with quasilinear preferences with respect to money[47]. The quasilinearity implies a cardinal utility measure that enables us to compute and compare overall welfare of different market structures. To obtain linear demand curves, we assume a quadratic utility function over every quantity of mail q_i^{rs} sent in segment s of region r through the network of operator i. Formally, we follow De Donder et al. (2001) and write total utility U as

$$U(q,m) = m + \sum_r \sum_s \left(a_I^{rs} q_I^{rs} - \frac{b^{rs}}{2}(q_I^{rs})^2 + a_E^{rs} q_E^{rs} - \frac{b^{rs}}{2}(q_E^{rs})^2 - eb^{rs} q_I^{rs} q_E^{rs} \right),$$

where $a, b, e > 0$ and m is the amount of money spent on other goods. The last term reflects the fact that the mail services offered by the two operators are not perfect

---

[47] Having in mind that most senders are businesses, quasilinearity is a reasonable assumption in the modeled riskless world. Businesses invest into mail as long as the NPV of an additional mailing is nonnegative, i.e. marginal utility of mail is greater than or equal to 1. Further, in an economy like Switzerland where postal consumption is small compared to total expenditure, postal consumption will be independent of the initial wealth endowment Y.

substitutes but rather differentiated products. The higher the degree of differentiation, the closer to zero is parameter e. Parameters a and b determine the market size and the slope of the demand curve.

A consequence of this utility specification is that demand in one market does not affect demand in another one. That is, cross-price elasticities between the market segments are zero and operators cannot increase demand in one market segment by serving an additional segment, i.e. no network externalities are directly included.

Utility maximization implies that our representative consumer satisfies with equality the budget constraint $\Sigma\Sigma(p_I^{rs} q_I^{rs} + p_E^{rs} q_E^{rs}) + m \leq Y$, where p_i^{rs} is the price the consumer has to pay to operator i for the mail product s delivered to region r. Y represents the initial wealth endowment of the economy. By computing the first-order conditions of the Lagrange function and solving the resulting equation system, we obtain the demand functions for the incumbent and the competitor as

$$q_i^{rs}(p_i^{rs}, p_j^{rs}) = \frac{1}{b^{rs}(1-e^2)}\left(a_i^{rs} - ea_j^{rs} - p_i^{rs} + ep_j^{rs}\right). \tag{7}$$

The slope of the demand curve in a given market is equal for both operators. Quantities are negatively related to the own price and positively to the price of the competitor ($\partial q_i/\partial p_i < 0$; $\partial q_i/\partial p_j > 0$). Furthermore, quantities increase with a higher degree of product differentiation (i.e., a smaller e).

On the *supply side*, pricing possibilities and cost structures determine profit functions. In the case of unregulated competition, where the incumbent and the entrant face no regulatory restrictions on pricing and production decisions, the operators are able to differentiate prices for every market segment and hence take into account demand properties specified in (7). We assume that there are no economies of scope between products, segments or regions. This assumption allows us to treat the production decision in each market segment independently.

Total costs per segment consist of a fixed and variable part. Entry occurs only if entrant E's earnings exceed variable costs cq and fixed costs F.[48] In contrast, the incumbent's fixed costs cannot be avoided (due to USO-obligations, the incumbent can not exit the market, cf. Section 3.8 for a discussion). The introduction of fixed costs is equivalent to increasing economies of scale and density. As we do not explicitly model

---

[48] This is a main difference in contrast to many existing entry models where entrants are assumed to behave as a competitive fringe with prices equal to marginal costs. See for example De Donder et al. (2006).

economies of scope, the market has the property of a natural monopoly especially in those segments where fixed costs are high.

4.2.3. Regulated Competition with Swiss licensing system

So far, there was no political or regulatory authority captured in the model. When such authorities set market rules, they usually change the underlying cost structures of the various operators. In Switzerland, the incumbent Swiss Post must provide universal service. This USO contains uniform tariffs across regions and service provision in every market segment[49]. Additionally, the reserved services (i.e. letters up to 100 gram) of Swiss Post have to finance a transfer T to cover the deficit in the postal offices[50]. If the incumbent does not break even due to cherry-picking entrants, the regulatory authority is entitled to charge licensing fees. Such fees are collected as a fixed fraction μ of the entrant's turnover. We treat μ as an exogenous parameter. Under such a regulatory regime, the profit functions in a given market segment are

$$\pi_I(p_I) = \sum_r \left[(p_I - c_I^r) q_I^r(p_I, p_E^r) + \mu \cdot p_E^r q_E^r(p_I, p_E^r) - F_I^r \right] - T,$$
$$\pi_E(p_E^r) = \sum_r \max\{0, (p_E^r(1-\mu) - c_E^r) q_E^r(p_I, p_E^r) - F_E^r\}. \tag{8}$$

Profit maximization yields $s(r+1)$ first-order conditions (FOC). Substituting the demand functions (7) into these first-order conditions, we obtain the reaction functions for the two operators. For the case of two regions D (dense) and R (rural), the two reaction functions in a given market segment s are

$$p_I(p_E^D, p_E^R) = \frac{b^R \left[a_I^D - ea_E^D + ep_E^D(1+\mu) + c_I^D \right] + b^D \left[a_I^R - ea_E^R + ep_E^R(1+\mu) + c_I^R \right]}{2(b^D + b^R)}$$
$$p_E^r(p_I) = \tfrac{1}{2}\left(a_E^r - ea_I^r + \tfrac{c_E^r}{(1-\mu)} + ep_I^r \right) \quad r \in \{D, R\}. \tag{9}$$

The incumbent's reaction function is much more complicated because it must average its price over the two regions. By solving this equation system, we obtain the equilibrium prices for each operator *given that entry occurs*, (i.e. the entrant's revenues exceed variable *and* fixed costs):

$$p_I = \frac{b^R \left[c_I^D + a_I^D - ea_E^D + \tfrac{e(1+\mu)}{2}\left(a_E^D - ea_I^D + \tfrac{c_E^D}{1-\mu}\right)\right] + b^D \left[c_I^R + a_I^R - ea_E^R + \tfrac{e(1+\mu)}{2}\left(a_E^R - ea_I^R + \tfrac{c_E^R}{1-\mu}\right)\right]}{(b^D + b^R)\left(2 - \tfrac{e^2(1+\mu)}{2}\right)}. \tag{10}$$

---

[49] We do not model all elements of Swiss Post's USO constraints. For a comprehensive overview of the current obligations faced by Swiss Post cf. PWC (2006b).

[50] Cf. Buser et al. (2008) for a detailed analysis.

Once this price is calculated, we obtain the price of the entrant by appropriately substituting this result into (9). If the entry condition is satisfied, the corresponding quantities can be calculated with the demand functions in (7).

If entry is not profitable at the incumbent's price in (10), the above formulae no longer hold. For example, if the entrant fails to break even in the dense area, the incumbent can improve its profits by increasing the price up to the limit at which the entrant just breaks even. Such a limit price p^{Limit} could be calculated as follows:

$$\pi_E(p_I^{Limit}, p_E^r(p_I^{Limit})) = 0 \Leftrightarrow p_I^{Limit} = a_I^r - \tfrac{1}{e}a_E^r + \tfrac{c_E^r}{e(1-\mu)} \pm \tfrac{2}{e}\sqrt{b^r \tfrac{1-e^2}{1-\mu} F_E^r}.$$

This 'opponent break even price' is limited by the monopoly price p^M. However, because of uniform pricing, any increase in the incumbent's price affects both regions and it is not clear how to balance the two different 'opponent break even prices' in every situation. In our simulation, we solve this problem numerically through appropriate use of the entrant's reaction and profit functions. With the resulting equilibrium prices, quantities and profits we can compute overall welfare by subtracting industry expenses from gross utility (due to quasilinear preferences). Doing so is equivalent to summing consumer net utility and the operators' profits.

4.2.4. Licensing fees lead to higher prices

Expressions (9) and (10) yield a first interesting result. Because the first derivative with respect to the licensing rate μ is positive under reasonable calibration, the incumbent will *increase* prices the more the regulator tries to finance the incumbent's USO through the licensing system. Intuitively, one would expect exactly the opposite. To see the intuition behind this result, we first study the impact of an increase in μ on the price of the entrant. To offset the negative effect of higher unit costs, the entrant must respond with an increase in prices; a higher licensing fee reduces the competitiveness of the entrant in equilibrium. Now the incumbent can charge a slightly higher price without losing any volume and thus further increases profits.

The financial effects to the incumbent can be identified by analyzing the marginal effect of μ on its profit function:

$$\frac{d\pi_I(p_I^*, p_E^*, \mu)}{d\mu} = \frac{\partial \pi_I}{\partial \mu} + \frac{\partial \pi_I}{\partial p_I}\frac{dp_I^*}{d\mu} + \frac{\partial \pi_I}{\partial p_E}\frac{dp_E^*}{d\mu} > 0.$$

The first term is the direct effect and represents the positive impact of the collected licensing fees. This direct effect equals $p_E q_E$ and is positive. The second and third terms represent indirect effects arising from price responses of both operators. The second term is zero at the optimum (because of the FOC). The third term is positive because both parts are positive (prices are strategic complements and both optimal prices increase with the license fee). We can therefore conclude that the incumbent's profits increase with a higher licensing fee. Thus, the licensing fee will help to sustain the USO, but will lead to a higher overall price level.

4.3 Calibration with Swiss Data

In order to predict price and welfare effects more precisely, we simulate the model using Swiss data. In Switzerland, geographic characteristics have a major impact on the cost structure of services. Differences in delivery time per household between dense and rural areas are significant and vary between delivery offices as much as 1:6. Accordingly, we divide the market into a dense region D and a rural region R.

To reflect the market structure we segment the market into five basic market segments s. The two basic sender groups, "businesses" and "households," can choose between two products "slow mail" and "fast mail." In addition, businesses have the option of mass mail. Crossing regions and segments yields ten submarkets.

4.3.1. Demand parameters

To estimate the demand functions (7) for each operator in each submarket, we must calibrate the parameters a and b with market data from 2003, when Swiss Post was still the only operator in the letter market and charged regulated prices. Rewriting (7) for the case of this regulated monopoly (RM) we get in every segment

$$q_{2003}(p_{2003}) = \frac{a_{RM} - p_{2003}}{b_{RM}} \text{ with price elasticity } \varepsilon_{2003} = -\frac{1}{b_{RM}} \frac{p_{2003}}{q_{2003}}. \quad (11)$$

After rearranging (11), we can directly calibrate parameter b with prices, quantities and elasticities from 2003.

Parameter a_i influences the size of the market of the two operator's services. By setting $a_I > a_E$, we can include effects like customer inertia, reputation effects, switching costs, or even quality differences like universal service provision that work in favor of the USP. Formally, we define x as the percentage of total demand the incumbent receives if the entrant were to offer the same price for its services. In the remainder of the chapter, we will refer to x as "incumbent advantage." For calibration we evaluate demand given in (7) at 2003 prices for both operators and solve the resulting equation system. We obtain

$$a_I = a_{RM}; \quad x = \frac{q_I}{q_I + q_E}; \quad p_I = p_E = p_{2003}$$
$$a_E = \frac{1}{1-e+\frac{e}{x}}\left(a_I(e-1+\tfrac{1}{x}) + p(1-e)(2-\tfrac{1}{x})\right)$$

Table 7 summarizes the major demand characteristics of the model. According to its 2003 annual report, Swiss Post delivered about 2.8 billion pieces of addressed mail, of which we assume 25% was destined to rural areas. The price elasticities are a delicate issue for two reasons. First, there is considerable divergence of opinion on the level. See Harding (2004) for an overview and Chapter 2 for a computation for aggregate Swiss mail data. Second, price elasticities determine the steepness of the demand curves; competition is more effective and leads to higher welfare results if price elasticities are greater, *ceteris paribus*. The most recent data of Swiss Post suggests that the values in Table 1 are overestimated. These reflect our assumptions based on estimations from former Swiss data and Chapter 2, studies from other countries, and industry experts. However, we expect mail elasticity to grow over time due to an increase of substitutes as shown in Chapter 2 (Figure 4). Therefore, we stay on the safe side with the overestimation. The main intuition behind the differences between segments is a substantially higher value per sent item for households (so businesses are more price sensitive), and an increasing variety of urgent communication possibilities such as e-mail resulting in a higher elasticity of fast mail compared to slow mail[51].

Table 7: Major demand characteristics

	Market size 2003	Prices 2003 (in €)[52]	Price elasticity	Incumbent advantage
Fast Mail B	21 %	0.56	-0.5	70 %
Fast Mail HH	6 %	0.60	-0.4	75 %
Slow Mail B	26 %	0.43	-0.4	65 %
Slow Mail HH	6 %	0.47	-0.3	70 %
Mass Mail B	39 %	0.33	-0.4	60 %

The incumbent advantage x is assumed to be higher for households than for businesses because of higher relative switching and information costs. The experiences

---

[51] This assumption is consistent with recent observations that customers are willing to switch to slow mail products after price increases.

[52] Throughout the book we assume an exchange rate of 1€ = 1.5 CHF.

from other liberalized postal, telecommunications or electricity markets support our assumptions; recent examples in Switzerland include Swiss Post in the parcels market.

4.3.2. Cost structure

For the production side of our little economy we estimate variable and fixed costs for collection, processing, delivery and overhead. This detailed attribution is somewhat artificial, as some economies of scale and scope get partially lost. Such effects could be included numerically, but then we could not compute unique equilibrium formulae anymore.

Table 8 shows how costs differ in the various market segments. In a first step, we map total costs based on data from Swiss Post's 2003 annual report onto processes (see Figure 10 for the postal value chain). Thereby we first corrected total cost by subtracting the € 234 million contribution that the addressed letter products paid last year to finance the postal outlet network's deficit. In line with empirical and technical estimations from comparable countries in Europe, Table 8 shows that delivery accounts for the largest portion of total costs (for average European values cf. Table 4).

In a second step, we attribute these process costs to market segments and regions. The figures are estimates and cannot reflect the economies of scope between the various segments and processes. Implicitly, we assume that collection costs are much higher for households and slightly higher for fast mail segments. Processing is slightly more expensive for fast mail but cheaper for mass mail because of extended presorting possibilities. Delivery costs are mainly determined by the quantity per segment and are slightly more expensive for fast mail and household segments. Overhead spreads equally over all segments.

Table 8: Major cost characteristics

	Collection	Processing	Delivery	Overhead
	10 %	30 %	55 %	5 %
Cost attribution to market segments				
Fast Mail B	15 %	20 %	24 %	20 %
Fast Mail HH	38 %	17 %	8 %	20 %
Slow Mail B	10 %	18 %	26 %	20 %
Slow Mail HH	30 %	16 %	6 %	20 %
Mass Mail B	7 %	29 %	36 %	20 %
	100 %	100 %	100 %	100 %
Fraction of variable costs				
Incumbent	50 %	80 %	40 %	10 %
Entrant	75 %	85 %	50 %	50 %

For the implemented scale effects, the fraction of fixed costs is important. In Switzerland, the number of letters per capita is the second largest in the world[53]. Hence, the total time the mail carriers need to reach the various delivery points is almost fixed and the economies of scale in delivery are large. For a detailed discussion and computation of economies of scale, density and scope the reader is referred to Chapter 3. In accordance with most of the literature (e.g. NERA 2004), we assume that processing costs are much more elastic. In total, about 50% of the incumbent's total costs are fixed. Compared to the incumbent, whose infrastructure is historically grown, designed for private customers and more capital intensive (postal outlets, sorting centers, delivery offices), the entrant's percentage of variable costs is higher.

So far, the main difference between the two operators was the entrant's lower fraction of fixed costs. According to current observations in the Swiss parcel market, competitors pay lower wages. As stated by the labor unions, the wage premium is currently around 16%[54] and hits the incumbent especially hard because about 80% of total costs are labor costs. The network design tailored to business customers further reduces the entrant's cost. We assume the upstream efficiency advantage (collection and presorting) of about 30% to reflect the savings realized by computerized sorting in the printing stage. In delivery, this advantage is much smaller (5%). Most business mailings are business-to-consumer. Consequently, one large customer causes a great deal of delivery points. Hence, a delivery network similar to that of the incumbent is needed with limited ways of cost innovation (the work is mainly physical). Nevertheless entrants can obtain cost savings by limiting themselves on just a view delivery days per week.

4.4 Results on Monopoly and on End-to-End Competition

With the calibrated model, we are now able to give some insight into the overall welfare consequences of various regulatory frameworks. In addition, we can perform sensitivity analysis and derive recommendations for postal operators on the strategies they should pursue under specific market rules. We focus on the first question and carry out sensitivity analysis only to judge the robustness of the results. In a first step, we evaluate the regulated monopoly of Swiss Post of 2003. Next, we analyze different forms of end-

---

[53] Depending on the data source Switzerland has the highest or second highest scale (behind the US). See Bundesnetzagentur (2006) for an overview based on UPU 2004 figures or PWC (2006b) for a recent assessment of the scale of Switzerland.

[54] Recent figures of PostReg (2005, 2006, 2007) indicate that Swiss Post's licensed competitors have a turnover of about CHF 60'000 per FTE. This is considerably less than Swiss Post's average labor cost in the letters section. Hence, the 16% could be well underestimated. PWC (2006b) assumes a labor cost advantage of about 25%.

to-end competition (complete liberalization without access possibilities) and change the introduced model slightly where needed. The monopoly scenarios serve primarily as a benchmark.

The quantitative results presented in this section serve as rough guidelines in which directions the examined regulatory regimes influence the market equilibrium in terms of prices, quantities, surpluses, and profits.

4.4.1. Monopoly: Positive effects of a price freeze

It is straightforward to evaluate the *regulated monopoly (RM)* of 2003, since the model was calibrated with data of 2003. Swiss post charged uniform prices at an average of 44 cents. With the underlying cost structure, the resulting loss was € 54 million, thus Swiss Post was close to break even despite of the USO. From now on, we will use this scenario as a benchmark reflecting the status quo[55].

As a second benchmark, we examine the case of an *unregulated monopoly (UM)*. What would happen, if the incumbent charged profit maximizing uniform prices? The results are interesting. The monopolist almost doubles its prices to 82 cents on average and thereby boosts its profit up to € 349 million. Profits are positive in all market segments except for fast mail for households in rural areas. However, the higher price level reduces consumer welfare dramatically: despite the high profit, a net welfare decrease of € -497 million results. Table 9 presents the details.

Table 9: Results monopoly cases

Legal Monopoly	Regulated	Unregulated
Average Price	0.44	0.82
Quantities (in Mio)	2836	1'787
Consumer Surplus	1491	591
Profit after transfer	-54	349
Welfare	1'437	940
Welfare change		-497

We conclude that Swiss Post did not charge monopoly prices in 2003[56]. For that reason, one could view the legal framework of 2003 as an effective price cap combined

---
[55] At this point, we note that there was a price increase in Switzerland in the beginning of 2004 due to the deficit in the postal network.
[56] Only if elasticities were assumed to be 3.5 times larger than the values in table 1, the model would predict monopoly pricing for Swiss Post in 2003.

with a break-even constraint. However, one does not know whether the regulated monopolist produced efficient.

4.4.2. End-to-end Competition: universal service at risk

In theory, competition leads to positive welfare effects mainly due to marginal cost pricing, improved efficiency, and product innovation. To reflect these potential benefits, we equipped the entrant with a substantial efficiency advantage. Additionally, we assume that the entrant improves product diversification, technically we set $e = 0.75$[57]. However, it is not clear for two main reasons, whether these positive effects lead to an increase in overall welfare. First, positive economies of scale diminish when entry occurs, so the market ends up with larger industry wide production costs. Second, the combination of a relatively inelastic demand with product differentiation possibilities could lead to oligopolistic pricing rather than marginal cost pricing. It will be interesting to see whether the model predicts prices above or below the ones from 2003.

In our first end-to-end competition case, hereafter referred to *"Regulated Competition (RC)"*, there are no restrictions on market entry. The incumbent must fulfill the universal service obligation as presented in Section 4.2. In return, the entrant must pay a licensing fee of 3% of its turnover. Table 10 depicts the results.

The model predicts an overall welfare decrease with universal service at risk. Despite an 18% increase in the overall price level, the incumbent's loss rises to about € 189 million. Entry occurs in all three dense business segments. Both operators make substantial profits with single-piece business mail. The incumbent reaches its best margins in rural business segments where no economies of scale and density are lost. The main losses occur in the household segments. The results are straightforward and support similar findings from Panzar (2001, 2002), Crew and Kleindorfer (2002), Dietl and Waller (2002), Waller (2001), and De Donder (2004).

The incumbent's main problem arises from the combination of universal service provision and uniform pricing. The entrant is able to undercut the incumbent in the dense segments and "picks the cherries," offered by the incumbent's tariff balancing act between the dense and rural region. This cherry-picking effect is much stronger than the cure for it, the licensing system. The entrant has to pay no more than € 15 million in licensing fees, a sum that represents less than 10% of its profits (and the incumbent's loss).

---

[57] In line with De Donder (2001) and Dietl and Waller (2002).

We observe a lot of price differentiation between the various market segments. Prices for households rise about 50%, whereas the average price in business segments rises about 10%, despite the entrant's cheaper prices.

Table 10: Results End-to-End Competition

Licensing Rate	Regulated (uniform pricing for I)			Unregulated (non uniform pricing)		
	$\mu = 0\%$	$\mu = 3\%$	$\mu = 20\%$	$\mu = 0\%$	$\mu = 3\%$	$\mu = 20\%$
Average Price (€)						
Incumbent	0.56	0.57	0.48	0.43	0.45	0.50
Entrant*	0.39	0.39	0.43	0.38	0.39	-
Average	0.49	0.50	0.48	0.43	0.44	0.50
Quantities (Mio #)						
Incumbent	1'652	1'631	2'408	2'540	2'503	2'571
Entrant	1'176	1'177	350	322	323	-
Total	2'828	2'808	2'759	2'863	2'826	2'571
Welfare (Mio €)						
Consumer Surplus	1'351	1'331	1'356	1'481	1'444	1'246
Profit I after transfer	-217	-196	-27	-124	-97	82
Profit Entrant	168	159	36	41	39	-
Welfare	1'302	1'294	1'365	1'398	1'386	1'328
Welfare change**	-135	-143	-72	-39	-51	-109
Other						
Licensing Fees (€)	-	14	30	-	4	-
Entry in # segments	3	3	1	1	1	-

* The values in this row represent weighted averages in active market segments.
** Values compared to the regulated monopoly case

One promising strategy for the USP against this kind of cherry picking is to abolish the uniform price. In such an *Unregulated Competition (UC)* the incumbent can differentiate its prices between regions. To implement this regulatory framework into the model, we make appropriate changes to expressions (2), (3) and (4). Doing so results in major change. The USP can now prevent entry in all segments except slow mail business. In the three market segments in which the entrant cannot enter anymore, we observe predatory behavior. The incumbent sets prices below the optimal prices in (4) to turn the entrant's profit into a deficit; the entrant cannot break even anymore and no entry occurs. The incumbent is better off because he defends 100% of the market. From this combination of predatory pricing and price discrimination between regions, consumers gain a € 100 million net surplus; the incumbent's prices are much lower on average, e.g. mass mailers gain about € 70 million net surplus (on the cost of rural regions).

Nevertheless, there are also losers, namely the entrant and the less price elastic households in rural areas where tariffs explode by more than 100%.

Compared to the regulated competition, the model predicts an overall welfare gain of € 92 million and a better financial situation for the incumbent. Still, the results are worse than in the case of the regulated monopoly of 2003. However, the welfare effects of this unregulated competition may be overestimated. There are several justifications for uniform pricing the model does not include. Examples are political reasons, menu and transaction costs, network externalities, and unwanted redistribution from rural regions and households to businesses, etc. We leave these extensions for further research. Table 10 summarizes the results.

4.4.3. Ambiguous effects of the licensing rate μ

For the above results, we assumed a licensing rate of 3%. If no licensing fee were collected ($\mu = 0\%$), the results would change only slightly. As predicted in Section 4.2.3, both operators offer lower prices. Consequently, the incumbent's loss rises by an additional € 21 million, which is more than the foregone licensing fees (€ 14 million). Thus, the indirect effect of the licensing system is in this case € 7 million (caused by price changes). The lower rate increases the entrant's potential profit margin, weakens the entry barrier function of the licensing system and leads to higher losses for the incumbent.

If the licensing rate is set to 20%, we observe a further important aspect of the licensing system. In the case of RC, we observe now only one market entry instead of three. The licensing system turns into a barrier to entry. In this special case, the entry barrier is desirable because the threat of entry forces the incumbent to charge low prices. As a result, overall welfare increases and the incumbent almost beaks even due to the indirect effect worth € 156 million (direct effect = additional 16 million). These good results are only one side of the coin, as we can see for the case of UC, where the incumbent's prices rise and welfare decreases. If the licensing rate is too high, the threat of entry is too low and the incumbent improves profits at the cost of overall welfare.

Figure 14 gives further insight into the mechanism of the licensing system. Under Regulated Competition, the incumbent breaks even with a licensing rate of 23%. Welfare is maximized at 26%. This is the point at which the entrant has to give up service even in the last segment (slow mail businesses). Still the threat of entry persists and sets the upper bound for the incumbent's prices. Any further rate increase would decrease the threat of entry and the incumbent (now a monopolist) can adjust his prices towards the profit maximizing unregulated monopoly solution.

Figure 14: Impact of the licensing rate on welfare and profits

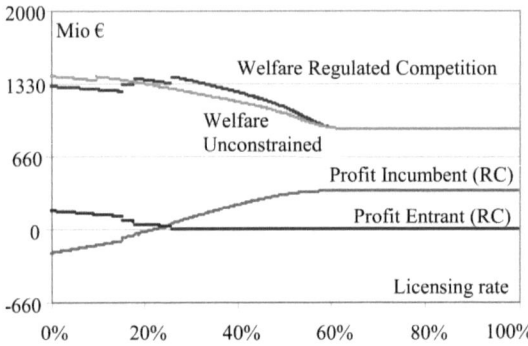

In the case of Unconstrained Competition, the optimal licensing rate is 0% where entry occurs in only one market segment. Up to a rate of 10%, the entrant stays in. At 10%, the incumbent is able to push the entrant out of the market by profitable predatory pricing. This discrete drop in prices yields the welfare jump that can be seen in the graph. From now on, any increase of the licensing rate reduces welfare.

4.4.4. Comparison of the four regulatory regimes and first conclusions

Having calculated overall price levels as well as the welfare of the different market rules, we are now able to make normative statements about which of the four scenarios a welfare-maximizing regulator should prefer. None of the competitive scenarios described above could reach the welfare of the Regulated Monopoly of 2003, even if a regulator maximized welfare with an optimal licensing rate. The model gives the following ordering in terms of welfare[58]:

$$RM \succ RC_{\mu^*=26\%} \succ UC_{\mu^*=0\%} \succ UM$$

If we apply these results to Switzerland, neither of the discussed competition scenarios is efficient. End-to-end competition does not necessarily lead to lower prices because of strategic interaction and the contested natural monopoly in delivery which yields a duplication of fixed costs. Welfare is likely to decrease, and Swiss Post's ability to fund its universal service obligation is heavily reduced. These conclusions include

---

[58] Only if elasticities are assumed at least 50% higher than the ones in Table 1, both competition scenarios turn out to be better than RM. As pointed out in section 3, the most recent market data rejects such high elasticity values.

positive effects of competition, such as higher product choice and a highly more efficient entrant.

In a dynamic context, Regulated "Competition" with a licensing rate between 20% and 25% might still be best because a profit-maximizing incumbent has direct incentives to reduce costs further. Suppose a regime in which the regulator reduces the licensing rate yearly by 1% for ten years. If the incumbent is able to reduce his costs appropriately, it can lower prices further to prevent a competitor's entry and thereby secure a 100% market share for exploiting the scale effects in distribution. From this point of view, a regulatory system similar to the one in Finland is reasonable.

There are various other ways to introduce competition in the letter market. One could relax universal service restrictions further, find other mechanisms for financing the USO (taxes, fixed licensing rates, last mile pricing, etc), introduce various forms of access regimes, copy US Worksharing, or combine the discussed competition designs with price cap regulation. The next section deals with two of those possibilities, namely price cap and Worksharing as a means to foster competition in the letter market.

4.5 Worksharing and Price Freeze Competition

Worksharing aims to minimize the costs of industry-wide service provision in the US letter market. The incumbent United States Postal Service (USPS) is granted a monopoly in delivery ("downstream monopoly"), whereas competitors can perform upstream services like collection and presorting just as well[59]. For these upstream services, USPS gives "worksharing discounts" on the official retail prices based on the avoided cost rule, depending on the value of the competitor's services for USPS. The system makes sense in economic terms if delivery has the property of a (contestable) natural monopoly and its innovation potential is limited in contrast to upstream services. Worksharing evolved over the last 30 years. In 2004, about 70% of total US mail volume was

---

[59] In fact, the USPS is granted a rigid monopoly that consists of two parts. (1) A reserved area for letters up to about 350 grams, and (2) a monopoly on recipients mail boxes. For example news papers companies are not allowed to deliver the daily newspaper into the mailbox. In terms of pricing the USPS is restricted not to grant worksharing discounts that exceed avoided costs. Hence, worksharing is essentially an outsourcing measure where competitors are given incentives by the USPS to perform upstream services whenever more efficient than the USPS. In this light, studies such as Kruse (2005) that conclude from analyzing US Worksharing that access should be introduced in the liberalized EU market are problematic. Such a combination of access and FMO has complex and potentially harmful effects in terms of USO financing. Further, incentive structures between operators are fundamentally changed. See Section 4.6 for a discussion.

workshared and the sum of all worksharing discounts totaled about US$ 14 Billion. Worksharing is fundamentally different from the European approach of market opening. Figure 15 opposes the two models.

Figure 15: EU market opening compared to US worksharing

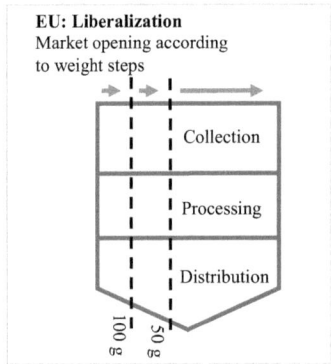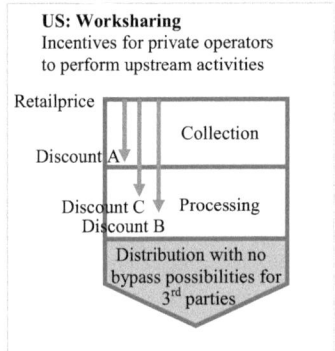

4.5.1. Modeling Worksharing

To compare *Worksharing (WS)* with the regulatory frameworks discussed above, some small changes of the model are needed. We change the demand side only to the extent that two calibration values are slightly changed. First, we reduce the incumbent advantage x in all segments by 50% (i.e. $x_{new} = \frac{1}{2}x_{old} + \frac{1}{4}$) because the entrant takes some advantage of the incumbent's downstream reputation and quality. Customers will switch faster to the entrant. Second, product differentiation possibilities are smaller because the entrant cannot deliver anymore. Therefore, we assume the product differentiation factor e to rise to 0.85. In other words, the two services of the two operators are still considered as two different products and demand is still described by (7).

The major changes are on the cost side, as the entrant is legally obliged to buy the downstream services from the incumbent. In return, the entrant receives a discount of δ^s (the "worksharing discount") for his collection and presorting efforts in market segment s[60]. In other words, the entrant pays the access price $A = p_I - \delta$ to the incumbent for final processing and delivery (see Figure 16). The entrant's variable costs for its upstream

---

[60] I.e. the modeled worksharing system is very stylized. In the US, there are various classes of worksharing discounts, and private operators need not to do all the upstream work as one block. They can specialize in any single discount.

activities are c_{Eu}, whereas the incumbent's variable costs split up in an upstream and downstream part, i.e. $c_I = c_{Iu} + c_{Id}$.

Figure 16: Stylized worksharing model

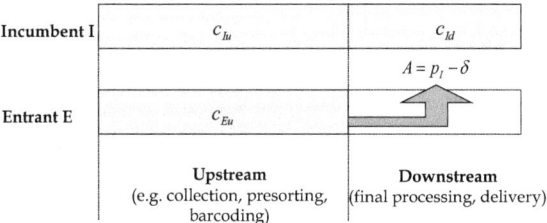

Since the universal service obligation can now be financed by the downstream monopoly, there is no reason for a licensing fee anymore, i.e. $\mu=0$. We thus rewrite the profit functions (8) as follows (for any given market segment):

$$\pi_I(p_I,\delta) = \sum_r \underbrace{\left(p_I - c_{Iu}^r - c_{Id}^r\right)q_I^r(p_I, p_E^r)}_{\text{End-to-End Mail}} + \underbrace{\left(p_I - \delta - c_{Id}^r\right)q_E^r(p_I, p_E^r)}_{\text{WorksharedMail}} - F_I^r - T,$$

$$\pi_E(p_E^r) = \sum_r \max\left\{0, \left(p_E^r - c_{Eu}^r - p_I + \delta\right)q_E^r(p_I, p_E^r) - F_{Eu}^r\right\}$$
(12)

4.5.2. US Worksharing – a Pareto Improvement

In the US, both retail prices and worksharing discounts are regulated. The Postal Rate Commission (PRC) is entitled to give its recommendations about pricing issues raised by the USPS[61]. Worksharing discounts are calculated using ECPR, where discounts equal USPS' cost savings for the respective worksharing activity ("avoided costs").

In the model, the incumbent's savings are exactly the upstream variable costs c_{Iu}. We rewrite (6) accordingly and set $c_{Iu} = \delta$ for the worksharing discount and $p_I = p_{2003}$ for the retail prices (i.e. again a price freeze to compare with the other price freeze scenarios). To obtain the profit-maximizing price for the entrant, we compute its first order condition. In equilibrium, optimal prices are

---

[61] Refers to the legislation up to 2006. Meanwhile, the PRC was renamed into Postal Regulatory Commission with new competences, the rate setting process was replaced by price cap regulation, but avoided costs for determining worksharing discounts was maintained.

$$p_I^* = p_{2003},$$
$$p_E^{r*} = \tfrac{1}{2}\left(a_E^r - ea_I^r + ep_{2003} + c_{Eu}^r + p_{2003} - c_{Iu}^r\right) \quad r \in \{D,R\}.$$ (13)

The results are straightforward. If entry occurs, there is a Pareto improvement compared to the Regulated Monopoly. The incumbent is indifferent whether to workshare or not and is better off if the entrant generates additional volume. Consumers only buy the products of the entrant if they gain net utility. The entrant can only enter if it charges lower prices due to more efficient production and/or it generates additional demand through product differentiation. In both cases, volumes increase when demand is downward sloping as assumed. Empirical findings from Cohen et al. (2002) support this argument.

In line with the theory, the model predicts an increase in overall volume of 2.2%. In total 640 million letters are workshared. The welfare improvement is € 77 million and the sum of worksharing discount totals € 97 million. Entry occurs in 5 segments (all business segments but rural fast mail). We note that these nice results do not hold anymore if worksharing discounts were set above avoided costs.

It is interesting to observe that the entrant charges a higher price than the incumbent does. Parameter analysis with different values for e shows that only for high values of e are the entrant's prices lower. I.e., only if the entrant cannot differentiate its products relative to the incumbent's ones, it must charge a lower price. If the entrant reaches to do product innovation, it might benefit from higher prices. In this case, consumers also benefit (their needs are better served) and, of course, so does the incumbent, who gets the additional volume for downstream delivery.

Table 11 presents detailed model results and illustrates the positive welfare and profit effects of a further increase in product differentiation.

The model supports the experience from the US: Successful entry occurs in business segments, the USP gains and can better sustain the USO at low prices. There is only one group, which is worse off, namely the workforce who represents the avoided upstream variable costs. However, they lose much less than in the case of regulated competition.

Table 11: Results Worksharing and Price Cap Competition

	US Worksharing		Price Cap Competition		
	$e = 0.85$	$e = 0.75$	$\mu = 0\%$	$\mu = 3\%$	$\mu = 20\%$
Average Price (€)					
Incumbent	0.44	0.44	0.44	0.44	0.43
Entrant	0.46	0.51	0.35	0.36	0.41
Average	0.45	0.46	0.41	0.41	0.42
Quantities (Mio #)					
Incumbent (*upstream)	2'291*	2'307*	2'073	2'079	2'432
Entrant	640	705	1'016	1'008	538
Total	2'932	3'012	3'090	3'088	2'970
Welfare (Mio €)					
Consumer surplus	1'515	1'533	1'612	1'610	1'560
Profit I after transfer	-22	-1	-300	-287	-165
Profit Entrant	21	48	90	79	21
Welfare	1'514	1'580	1'402	1'402	1'416
Welfare change (RM)	+77	+143	-35	-35	-21
Welfare change (RC)			+100	+108	+51
Other					
Discounts/Fees (Mio €)	97	118	0	10	44
Entry in # segments	5	7	3	3	2

4.5.3. Price Freeze Competition

The two end-to-end competition cases from Section 4.4 yield much lower overall welfare than worksharing. One reason is the price-driving effect of the licensing system. To offset this price-driving effect, we supplement the RC case with a price freeze.

Table 11 reports the results of such a *"Price Cap Competition."* The price freeze has a positive effect on overall welfare compared to the Regulated Competition case (but not compared with the Regulated Monopoly) because the overall price level drops. The incumbent is worse off. He has no further possibility of responding competitively and its deficit increases up to € 287 million – the USO burden is not covered at all. Once again, this regulatory regime is not feasible for Switzerland from a legal point of view. Similar to the findings in Section 4.4, only a sufficient high licensing rate can stabilize the financial situation of the USP. It prevents entry, and if the rate is set accordingly, it gives the incumbent incentives to reduce costs and to avoid potential entry.

4.5.4. Discussion

Both the regulatory regimes presented in this section did help to improve overall welfare compared to the competition cases examined in Section 4.4. However, Price Cap Competition is desirable for consumers (higher net utility), but not for the ones who must pay the higher burden of the universal service obligation. If this burden would have to be paid by the consumers through a special postal tax, they are again worse off compared to the Regulated Monopoly of Swiss Post in 2003.

In contrast, Worksharing seems to be the only system that can improve economic efficiency in the sector. Worksharing realizes the benefits of competition without sacrificing the economies of scale and density in delivery and putting universal service at risk.

Figure 17: Development of overall mail volumes in selected high-volume countries

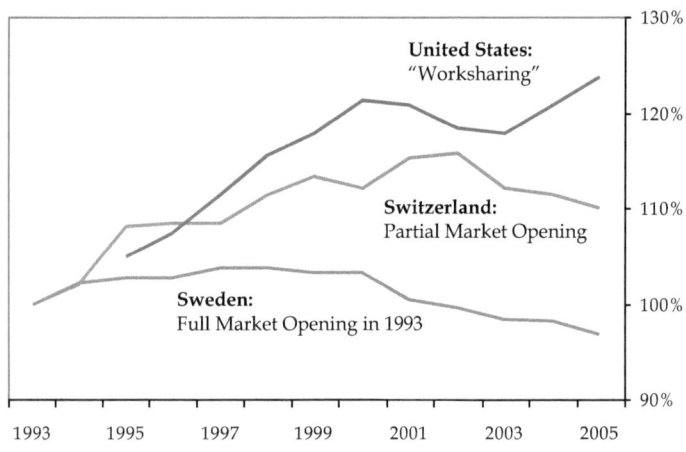

Source: PTS, Swiss Post, UPS

Empirically, one could try to find out how tariffs and volumes do vary between the different regulatory regimes applied in practice today. The model predicts that the United States should have large volumes per capita ceteris paribus. In liberalized markets, postal operators should have problems sustaining the USO due to smaller volumes. In regulated monopolies (or licensing regimes with very high rates) tariffs and volumes should lie somewhere in between. However, such a comparison is difficult because demand and supply factors as well as USO-requirements vary heavily across nations. Figure 17 shows the development of overall mail volumes in Sweden, Switzerland, and the US (all three countries exhibit very high volumes per capita). The figure provides some[62] empirical support of our model findings.

4.6 Access with Bypass

We discussed various scenarios of end-to-end competition, and also Worksharing which can be seen as a regulated access scenario, where in fact just the process of determining access prices is regulated. I.e., access prices or worksharing discounts are computed by the USPS according to the Avoided Costs rule[63] and approved by the regulatory commission PRC.

We saw that end-to-end poses some problems, but Worksharing improves the situation. Why not just combine the two? This combination is referred to as "access with bypass" and enables competitors to "piecemeal bypass" the incumbent (see Figure 10 for a graphical illustration). A recent application in practice is the United Kingdom, where downstream access prices are regulated and the market is completely open. Yet, it is two early to draw conclusions from the UK case, as it lacks both the long term perspective (full market opening as of 2006) and a level playing field; the incumbent Royal Mail still enjoys a value added tax (VAT) advantage. Whereas private competitors must charge VAT on their products, Royal Mail is exempt.

We leave a simulation within our model framework for future research. However, there are already many economic papers on the subject, thereof a vast majority pointing into the same direction. Among others, Panzar (2004) and De Donder (2006) discuss the issue in a setting with full market opening, customer direct access, and regulated access prices. I.e. customers have the choice between the incumbent's retail products, the incumbent's wholesale products, and services of new competitors. These new entrants have the choice of providing end-to-end services, consolidation (upstream services), and if needed, of selectively bypassing the incumbents network by setting up own distribution networks where the entrant's delivery costs are lower than the incumbent's access prices. The main difference of the two papers is that Panzar minimizes uniform retail prices, whereas De Donder maximizes welfare. The main message of the two papers remains the same. "Piecemeal bypass poses more problems than end-to-end bypass", i.e. end-to-end competition is preferable to regulated access with bypass scenarios. Even more, both

---

[62] Note that the different development could have been caused by other country specific factors too. We leave a detailed analysis for future research.

[63] equals ECPR (Efficient component pricing rule)

papers obtain the best welfare measures for regulated access scenarios without bypass, which economically comes closest to the US Worksharing model.

Similar results provide Armstrong (2001, 2006b), Billette de Villemeur et al. (2004a, 2004b), Crew and Kleindorfer (2002, 2003, 2004, 2006a), De Donder et al. (2004), Calzada (2005), Gautier (2006), Plaut/Frontier (2007), and PWC (2006a, 2006b). The latter and Crew and Kleindorfer (2002, 2004) point out that in such a setting, uniform access prices worsen the situation compared to a zonal access pricing regime. Based on their simulation study, Crew and Kleindorfer (2006a) note that "prohibiting bypass yielded greater welfare than any of the cases that allowed bypass". Armstrong (2006b) concludes that under bypass some form of output taxes for entrants would be needed to prevent inefficient entries. We conclude that – at least in theory – piecemeal bypass yields negative effects on welfare and decreases the financial power of universal service providers to sustain the USO.

The underlying reasoning is, that combining end-to-end competition with some form of downstream access, where entrants can hand over mail to the incumbent's delivery network if wanted, will provide entrants with *additional possibilities of cherry picking* by focusing on processes (in addition to customers and regions), thereby eroding the concept of uniform prices (and thus universal service) as operators either align prices to costs or lose market share. This mechanism would most probably also hold in Switzerland, where market entry barriers for piecemeal bypass are particularly low because of high mail volumes per capita. PWC (2006b) supports this argument. Hence, Switzerland should, in the presence of (asymmetric) universal service obligations, not introduce "access with bypass" regulations, i.e. combine full market opening policies with a regulated access regime (be it ex ante or ex post).

4.7 Conclusions

Like the member states of the European Community, Switzerland is in the process of liberalizing its domestic postal markets. In 2004, a new postal ordinance fully opened the parcels market by introducing end-to-end competition using a licensing system to help the incumbent fund its universal service obligation.

We asked, what would happen if the letter market were liberalized in the same way? To gain deeper insight on this issue, we adapted a price competition framework from De Donder et al. (2001), tailored it to Swiss circumstances and extended it further to include worksharing. The model enables quantitative comparisons between monopoly, competition and worksharing scenarios. Despite the limits of such a quantitative model, we believe that the main results are robust and straightforward.

We identify US Worksharing[64] as a Pareto improvement compared to monopoly regulation. Moreover, our model predicts higher welfare and much better USP stability than various ways of end-to-end competition with different levels of licensing rates. End-to-end competition with its full liberalization of the postal value chain is leading to serious difficulties for the incumbent to sustain the universal service requirements. The more restrictions are imposed on the incumbent's pricing flexibility (uniform price, price freeze), the worse becomes the financial situation of the incumbent.

We conclude that Switzerland should be very cautious when copying European plans of end-to-end competition. We believe caution is especially indicated when the assumption of high economies of scale and density in delivery truly reflects the industry (the results in Chapter 3 strongly underpin this presumption). Our model predicts that complete letter market liberalization will lead to higher prices, to much more price differentiation between regions and customers (in favor of business customers and cities), to an erosion of universal service due to Swiss Post's attempts to adapt its business model to the underlying market forces and to continuous financial problems of the incumbent. These problems will even tighten, if a full market opening was combined with an access regime under which competitors could use the incumbent's delivery network when needed. We leave an evaluation within our model for further research.

The model cannot cope with some dynamic advantages of competition. For example, there were no possibilities for Swiss Post for dynamic efficiency gains over time. If one believes those efficiency potentials to be large, end-to-end competition could still be a

---

[64] The Pareto improvement is only achieved if retail prices stay regulated *and* worksharing discounts are equal or less to avoided costs.

desirable solution. However, postal services already face increasing indirect competition through digital means of written communication (cf. Figure 9 page 23). The overall volume in single-piece mail is shrinking in most highly developed countries, including Switzerland despite growing written communication markets. This rapidly evolving "e-competition" threatens the postal services as end-to-end competition does. Regulated "monopolists" and worksharers are "hit" only once, whereas incumbents competing in fully liberalized letter markets are "hit" twice.

5. Pricing in Liberalized Two-Sided Mail Markets

5.1 Introduction

So far we have considered the postal market being a "one-sided market". The results from Section 4 as well as probably any reference so far assumed implicitly that the recipients of mail do not affect mail demand at all. Yet, virtually any mail piece is basically written communication between *two* parties and hence it is not a priori clear whether we can exclude the recipient-side from our analysis. Recent developments in economic theory have pointed to a broad range of so called "two-sided markets" where platforms link two or more groups of consumers. Examples include stock exchanges (investors and listed companies), internet search engines (internet users and advertisers), or night clubs (males and females).

Postal operators can be seen as such platforms between senders/mailers on one side and receivers/recipients on the other. A first analysis that incorporates the recipient side into the modeling exercise was undertaken by Felisberto, Finger, Friedli, Krähenbühl and Trinkner (2006). The model was further developed in Friedli, Jaag, Krähenbühl, Nielsen, Pihl and Trinkner (2006). The authors analyze the effect of the introduction of a two-part tariff that consists of variable postage paid by senders and a fixed "delivery flat rate" that recipients must pay in case they prefer doorstep delivery over free P.O. box delivery. Figure 18 illustrates the proposed pricing for which the authors find mixed effects on overall welfare.

Figure 18: Illustration of a possible two-part tariff in the postal sector

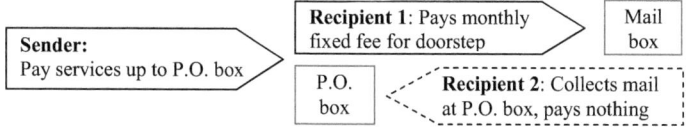

If letters are a means of communication between two parties, at least one of the two parties has a positive willingness to pay. Postal operators offer the service that exploits this willingness to pay. Interestingly, virtually all postal operators apply a pre-paid mechanism that goes back on Rowland Hill's proposal of charging only the sender-side of the market instead of the receivers too. However, the pre-paid mechanism of today involves the potential for the senders to bill the postage onward to the receivers. This potential varies between the various classes of mail and is essentially determined by the bargaining position between the two communicating parties. Postage for advertising mail remains on the sender-side, while postage in commercial relationships is usually – directly or indirectly – passed on to the receivers. E.g., Swiss banks increasingly bill postage for bank statements directly to their clients (i.e. the receivers).[65]

The fact that mail consists of two parties communicating with each other over a choice of platforms (postal operators) makes the postal market *potentially two-sided*. If this two-sided market is served by only one operator (as it remains the predominant regulation in most countries) the designated postal operator has the necessary bargaining power to choose the pricing mechanism of her choice (sender pays, receiver pays, or a mix between the two as analyzed by Felisberto et al. (2006) and Friedli et al. (2006). Yet, senders and receivers are able to reallocate postage by means of negotiation as mentioned above.

In competitive markets, two effects could potentially lead to different optimal pricing principles: (a) the historical operator loses its market power on the sender side because of competing networks, and (b) receivers get bargaining power in terms of whom to give the right to operate their P.O. box. The latter effect could in principle yield a situation where large receivers prefer P.O. boxes over mail boxes as the former give them the possibility sell their address exclusively in license to a specific operator.

In this chapter we analyze whether the traditional pricing concept (sender pays principle) remains dominant in competitive postal markets. To do so, we split the postal market in a processing and delivery part, where a postal operator faces two kinds of customers: senders in the former and receivers in the latter part of the market. Based on the contributions by Laffont, Rey and Tirole (1998), Rochet and Tirole (2003), Armstrong (2006a) and Panzar (2006) we develop a theoretical model with consumers' platform choice between two operators competing in linear upstream and two-part downstream prices and being interconnected by a symmetric access regime to P.O. boxes. Thereby, we extend the analysis of a delivery flat rate by Felisberto et al. (2006) and Friedli et al. (2006) to a competitive environment and assess optimum pricing schemes in market equilibrium.

The paper builds mainly on Jaag and Trinkner (2008a) and is structured as follows. Section 5.2 discusses the background on the theory of two-sided markets and its relevance for postal markets. Section 5.3 presents the model outline. Section 5.4 provides a rough

---

[65] Often, the official single-peace tariff is billed instead of the reduced business rate.

calibration of the model and presents the derived optimal pricing structure for the two-sided P.O. box market. We conclude in Section 5.5.

5.2 Background – is the postal market two-sided?

In two-sided markets, platforms enable the interaction of two or more groups of agents, where the surplus of one group of agents depends on the number of users that are connected to the platform on the other side (Armstrong 2006a). Real world examples of such two-sided markets with multiple platforms include many internet applications, the credit card industry, radio or television broadcasting, peer-to-peer networks, computer operating systems, or telecommunication networks. A precise *definition of a two-sided market* is given by Rochet and Tirole (2005) and depends mainly on its pricing properties:

> "Consider a platform charging per-interaction charges a_B and a_S to the buyer and the seller sides. The Market for interactions between the two sides is one-sided if the volume V of transactions realized on the platform depends only on the aggregate price level $a = a_B + a_S$, i.e. is insensitive to reallocations of this price between the buyer and the seller. If by contrast V varies with a_B while a is kept constant, the market is said to be two-sided."

Hence, postal services would not satisfy the definition of two-sided markets in case mail demand remained the same if postage was charged to receivers instead of senders.

Two-sided markets are strongly linked with *network externalities*.[66] Rochet and Tirole (2003) note, 'many if not most markets with network externalities are two-sided'. Armstrong (2006a) even includes (cross) network externalities in his definition of two-sided markets: the number of subscribers of one group increases the surplus of the other one. Consequently, for virtually any (two-sided) platform, attaining the critical mass on both sides of the market is the core of the business with pricing being one of the most crucial success factors to overcome the chicken-and-egg problem involved when setting up a new platform. From this point of view, two-sided markets can be seen as the subset of markets with network externalities, where the allocation of prices among the various groups of agents affects the degree of exploitation of those externalities. This in turn is the case, if the platforms pricing policy cannot be offset by private redistribution between the various groups of agents. In postal markets for example, where postage predominantly is charged directly to the senders, often receivers finally pay the postage, as senders bill it

---

[66] Network externalities arise if the utility that a given user derives from joining a network depends upon the number of other users who are in the same network. Positive network externalities are present if a customers' utility of a good or service is an increasing function of the number of other users.

onwards (e.g. distance selling). Hence, it is not a priori clear, if the postal market is two-sided.

5.2.1. Pricing structures in two-sided markets

In two-sided markets, we often observe pricing structures in which one side (one group of agents) heavily cross-subsidizes the other side of the market. Internet search engines provide their core business (searching the internet) for free, radio and TV channels are free of charge, and credit card holders even get fringe benefits for the frequent use of their card. Table 11 provides an overview of pricing structures in selected two-sided industries.

At a first glance, the cross-subsidization is astonishing as both sides in each of those markets derive a positive utility of the platform and thus in principle would have a positive willingness to pay. Yet, those pricing policies persist even in mature markets, and it appears dominant in competitive two-sided markets not to exploit the willingness to pay on one side of the market.

Table 12: Overview of pricing structures in two-sided markets

	Credit Card	Search engine	Electronic Document viewing	Mobile	Direct Mail
Side 1: Originator	Payer (Buyer)	Searcher	Reader	Caller	Sender (Advertiser)
Pricing	**Small or zero** subscriber fee, **fringes** with use	**Free**	**Free** (zero license charge for adobe reader)	Per minute, subscriber fee	Per peace charge
Platform (Examples)	American Express, Visa, Mastercard	Google, Yahoo!	Adobe Writer and Reader	Mobile networks	Postal operators
Side 2: Enabler	Payee (Seller)	Content provider / Advertiser	Content providers	Receiver	Receiver
Pricing	Subscriber fee, % of transaction amount,	Price per hit	Licensing costs	Mostly **free**, subscriber fee	**Free**

In general, the cross-subsidization aims at establishing a consumer base that as a whole can be sold to a group of individual commercial agents aiming to sell products to this consumer base. Thus, most two-sided markets are in effect intermediaries that derive their economic value by reducing transaction costs or information asymmetries (mostly between sellers and potential buyers). To get the critical mass and resolving the typical chicken-and-egg problem, the dominant strategy appears to heavily cross-subsidize one group of agents either directly (low, zero or even negative price) or indirectly through tying a valuable product (free internet query, free radio broadcasting) with a product establishing negative network externalities (advertisement).

Very close to the latter interpretation and related to the formal resolution of two-sided market models, two-sided markets can be seen as ordinary markets with the product being the provision of a client base which exhibits acquiring expenses equalling the loss on a second product offered to that client base. Thereby, acquiring takes place indirectly by offering a valuable, subsidized service (free internet query). In most of the cases, this valuable product inhibits substantial economies of scale (and only indirect network externalities over the other side of the market) which in turn reduce acquiring cost per client, whereas the marginal indirect revenue remains constant. Consequently, two-sided markets are heavily concentrated.

5.2.2. Two-sidedness of the postal market

We now turn to the important question whether postal markets are two-sided markets according to the definition of Rochat and Tirole (2005) cited above.

Today, in most postal markets it is secured that any address is connected to the postal network by means of the "universal service obligation" that obliges as least one postal network to provide "universal access" for universal services such as letters and parcels and to deliver that service to any address throughout the country. Thus, by regulation, network externalities are secured. Additionally, universal providers are – for example in Switzerland – by law not allowed to charge the receiver's for connecting them to net network. Even New Zealand, where the postal market is since a decade fully liberalized and universal service was reduced to its basics, forbids in its "deed of understanding" with New Zealand Post a "rural delivery fee" aimed at residents in remote areas. Those universal service definitions indicate that senders exhibit a positive network externality if everybody is connected to the postal network.

However, it is not yet clear whether total demand is affected by a change in the pricing structure, for example if postage was to be paid by receivers instead of senders at it was the case before the reform of Rowland Hill. History on the reform of Rowland Hill reveals that demand virtually exploded after the change in the price structure. Thus, we have a first indication of the two-sidedness of the postal market.

Research by Felisberto et al. (2006) on the receiver pays principle in the postal sector analyzes the effects of the introduction of a delivery flat rate, where receivers are given the choice between free P.O. box delivery and costly last mile doorstep delivery (in the form of a yearly flat rate). [67] This would enable a monopolistic platform to reduce senders' tariffs. By exclusion of a rebalancing between the two groups of agents behind the scenes and by assumption that P.O. box switchers originate the same amount of mail as before, positive demand effects were found.

More recent research by Friedli et al. (2006) on the delivery flat rate indicates that up to 35% of the customers switching to P.O. box delivery would not anymore empty their mail box. This would cause a significant drop in mail volumes. This survey points towards the presence of two-sidedness in the postal market.

A similar argument is the following. If the receiver was about to pay, the sender has no guarantee that the receiver accepts the mail (for example, paying postage for accepting unwanted direct mailings). Receivers would most probably reject unwanted mail, which in turn postal operators would send back to the senders by charging them accordingly. This would reduce response rates clearly and reduce the amount of direct mail sent as observed in Chile.

A contrary argument might be that most senders of transactional mail bill their postage onwards to the receivers. Thereby, single peace tariffs instead of (lower) business customer tariffs are charged. Thus, receivers perceived cost might reduce if postal operators would bill the postage directly to the receivers (positive demand effect).

We conclude that there exists large evidence that postal markets indeed are two-sided. This was first recognized by Panzar (2006). Our main contribution to the literature is the formalization of a competitive two-sided postal market which we calibrate to yield robust results on optimal pricing strategies.

5.3 A two-sided postal market model

Our two-sided postal market model consists of two groups of agents, namely senders and receivers of mail, and two platforms (postal operators) linking the senders and the receivers. Senders choose over whom to hand over their mail, whereas receivers have the

---

[67] Jaag (2007) discusses the welfare effects associated with the consumers' choice between costly doorstep delivery and free delivery to a P.O. box.

possibility to grant special delivery rights to one of the two operators[68]. The assumption of special rights involves the necessity of interconnection of the two operators; In order to offer end-to-end service to her sender, a postal operator needs access to the other's delivery network. Otherwise, an operator would not be able to reach P.O. box addresses operated by the other one. We are primarily interested, how different interconnection rates affect the platforms pricing strategies, thus we treat access prices as exogenous and provide in Section 5.4 sensitivity analysis. For simplicity reasons, we assume reciprocal access pricing.

Thus, there are two sides in the postal market: Upstream, postal operators compete for sending customers; downstream, they compete for receiving customers. We follow Laffont, Rey and Tirole (1998) in the modeling of network competition and link the postal upstream market on the sender's side to a downstream market for local delivery monopolies.

Figure 19: Model outline

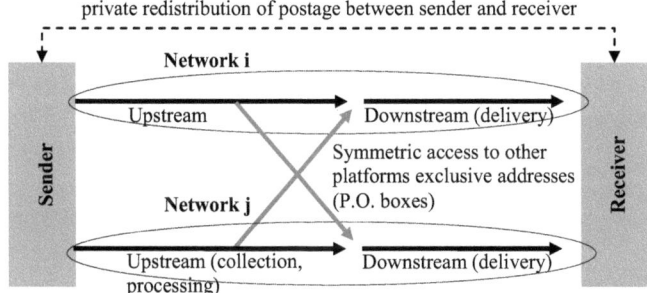

Figure 19 provides a graphical representation of the model outline. In our model, total mail demand is a function of the sum of the sender's price p_u and the receiver's price p_d per item. Total volume is determined by the sender primarily, but we assume that through private redistribution (as observed in practice) the receiver influences the sender's communication channel and vice versa. We include the possibility that the operators' optimal behavior leads to an interdependence of these prices and a delivery flat rate, such

---

[68] In most countries, receivers have the choice between a free doorstep delivery and (sometimes costly) P.O. box. It is important to note that as soon as a P.O. box is chosen, the P.O. box operator obtains the exclusive rights for final delivery into the P.O. box. In this view, the assumption could reflect the subset of mail destined to P.O. boxes, or a regulation where every household appoints the operator of her choice as its exclusive delivery carrier.

that total volume is sensitive to reallocations of the total price. Hence, the model qualifies as a two-sided market (with multihoming).

As opposed to e.g. the telecommunications market, the two user bases (senders, receivers) are not necessarily linked together: A subscriber for delivery services with one operator does not predetermine the operator choice when sending a letter (P.O. box holders can still send the mail with other carriers). However, downstream market share affect both cost structure and downstream income, which determines competitive behavior upstream.

In both parts of the market, consumers can chose between two competing networks i and j, which are differentiated à la Hotelling. Given income y and mail consumption q, a consumer (sender / receiver) located at x and joining network i has utility

$$U = y + v - t_m |x - x_i| + u(q).$$

We assume that consumers are uniformly distributed over the interval [0,1] and the two networks are located at the extremes. t_m is a market-specific parameter for the substitutability of the two competing networks and determines the degree of disutility a sender perceives from the network offering services that do not exactly meet the senders preference x. Thus, a consumer located at $x = 0.5$ is just about equally dissatisfied by the two operators i and j located at $x_i = 0$ and $x_j = 1$ and finds herself indifferent. Following Laffont, Rey and Tirole (1998) we define sender gross surplus $U_u(q)$ by

$$U_u(q) = \beta^{\frac{1}{\eta}} \frac{q^{1-\frac{1}{\eta}}}{1-\frac{1}{\eta}}$$

We allow for *redistribution* of tariffs between senders and receivers by specifying the total quantity as a function both of the senders price p_u *and* the receivers price p_d. If for example a bank client orders the monthly bank statement knowing that the postage will be charged on her bank account, receivers generate the mail, and the senders price still affects mail volumes although they do not actually pay for it. Similarly, if the client was charged a reception fee, this would again affect senders demand. Hence, sender's utility maximization yields total demand

$$q = \beta \cdot (p_{u,i} + \zeta p_{d,i})^{-\eta}$$

with constant price elasticity of demand -η. ζ reflects to what *degree* customers can redistribute postage by means of private negotiation and hence, to what degree senders take into account the receiver price. With ζ close to 0, senders' demand is independent of the receiver price (resulting from the lack of negotiation between senders and receivers). $\zeta = 1$ yields a situation where the sender maximizes over the aggregate *variable* price level, irrespective of the tariff structure. However, the market still qualifies the two-sided markets property as long as the fixed downstream reception fee P_d is nonzero (in the literature referred to as "delivery flat rate"). For $P_d = 0$, senders and receivers would be able to redistribute (pass through) charges behind the scene completely to the very same level irrespective of the operators' pricing strategies.

The total cost for end-to-end postal service consists of a fixed part f_m in both the upstream ($m=u$) and downstream markets ($m=d$) and quantity-dependent variable cost c_m:

$$C = f_u + f_d + q \cdot (c_u + c_d).$$

The operators' profit functions are then given by

$$\pi_i = \max_{p_{u,i}, p_{d,i}, P_{d,i}} \left\{ \begin{array}{l} \alpha_{u,i}\alpha_{d,i}[(p_{u,i} + p_{d,i} - c_{u,i} - c_{d,i})q(p_{u,i} + \zeta p_{d,i}) - f_u - f_d + P_{d,i}] \\ + \alpha_{u,i}(1 - \alpha_{d,i})[(p_{u,i} - a - c_{u,i})q(p_{u,i} + \zeta p_{d,j}) - f_u] \\ + (1 - \alpha_{u,j})\alpha_{d,i}[(p_{d,i} + a - c_{d,i})q(p_{u,j} + \zeta p_{d,i}) - f_d + P_{d,i}] \end{array} \right\}, \quad (14)$$

where $\alpha_{m,i}$ is market share of operator i in market m. Hence, a postal operator's profit consists of three parts: The first part is due to letters she processes end-to-end. The second and the third ones relate to mails which originate in the own network and which are delivered through the other operator's network, and vice versa.

To solve the model, we derive the competitive outcome in the two sides of the postal market consecutively. Thereby, the model is solved backwards in order to find subgame perfect equilibria. In a first step, we analyze upstream competition in non-discriminatory linear tariffs, where the two networks compete for senders and yield optimal prices and market share in the upstream market as a function of equilibrium downstream prices and market shares. In a second step, we derive optimal two-part pricing structures[69] of the downstream market, i.e. competition for P.O. box subscribers.

We focus on parameter constellations, in which there exist unique and symmetric equilibria in both the upstream and downstream markets (cf. Laffont, Rey and Tirole, 1998, propositions 1 and 7).

---

[69] I.e. the pricing for P.O. boxes consists of a fixed and a variable part where both parts can be positive (receiver pays), negative (receiver obtains) or zero (no money flow in either direction).

5.3.1. Upstream competition in non-discriminatory linear tariffs

We start our analysis with upstream competition, where postal operators compete for quantity. At that stage, downstream prices p_d^*, P_d^* and market shares α_d^* are given from downstream competition and are symmetric. Under the assumption of uniform and non-discriminatory pricing (i.e. the postal operator is not able to discriminate mail by destination), the sender's net surplus in the upstream market is

$$v_u(p_u, p_d^*) = \max_{q_u}\{U_u(q) - (p_u + \zeta p_d^*)q\} = \beta \frac{(p_u + \zeta p_d^*)^{-(\eta-1)}}{\eta - 1}$$

Operator i's market share is therefore

$$\alpha_{u,i} = \alpha_{u,i}(p_{u,i}, p_{u,j}) \equiv \frac{1}{2} + \sigma_u[v_u(p_{u,i} + \zeta p_d^*) - v_u(p_{u,j} + \zeta p_d^*)]$$

where $\sigma_u \equiv \frac{1}{2t_u}$ is an index of substitutability resulting from the location of the senders and the operators.

In symmetric equilibrium, we have $\alpha_{d,i}^* = \alpha_{u,i}^* = 0.5$, $p_{u,i}^* = p_{u,j}^* = p_u^*$ and $p_{d,i}^* = p_{d,j}^* = p_d^*$. The first-order condition of (14) with respect to p_u is

$$\frac{1}{4}[(p_u + p_d^* - c_u - c_d)q' + q] + \frac{1}{2}\frac{\partial \alpha_{u,i}}{\partial p_u}[(p_u + p_d^* - c_u - c_d)q(p_u + \zeta p_d^*) - f_u - f_d + P_{d,i}^*]$$
$$+ \frac{1}{4}[(p_u - a - c_u)q' + q] + \frac{1}{2}\frac{\partial \alpha_{u,i}}{\partial p_u}[(p_u - a - c_u)q(p_u + \zeta p_d^*) - f_u]$$
$$+ \frac{1}{4}[(p_d^* + a - c_d)q' + q] - \frac{1}{2}\frac{\partial \alpha_{u,i}}{\partial p_u}[(p_d^* + a - c_d)q(p_u + \zeta p_d^*) - f_u] = 0$$

Note that a unit increase in price lowers market share by σ_u times quantity per customer: $\partial \alpha_{u,i}/\partial p_{u,i} = -\sigma_u q$ and a unit loss of market share leads to the loss of the per-customer profit. In analogy to equation (8) in Laffont, Rey and Tirole (1998), the first-order condition can be rewritten as

$$\frac{p_u^* - \kappa}{p_u^*} = \frac{1}{\eta}[1 - 2\sigma_u \pi(p_u^*, p_d^*, P_d^*)],$$

where $\kappa = c_u + \dfrac{a + c_d - p_d^*}{2}$ is perceived direct marginal cost and

$$\pi(p_u, p_d, P_d) = \frac{1}{2}[(p_u + p_d - c_u - c_d)q(p_u + \zeta p_d) - f_u - f_d + P_d]$$

is per-customer profit when the two networks charge identical prices.

5.3.2. Downstream competition in two-part tariffs

In upstream competition, downstream prices p_d^*, P_d^* and market shares α_d^* have been taken as given. They are determined in downstream competition, where postal operators compete for market share. Again, differentiation is à la Hotelling. Thereby, operators can build local monopolies, which strengthen their market power upstream. Receiver net surplus from chosen network i is

$$w_{d,i} = v_{d,0} + v_d(p_{d,i}) - P_{d,i}.$$

Receiver surplus net of per-piece price $p_{d,i}$ is in analogy to above denoted by v_d. We introduce the term $v_{d,0}$ to assure that every receiver is interested in joining one of the two delivery networks. Since a fraction ζ of this price is passed on to senders, we have

$$v_d(p_{d,i}) = U_d(q) - (1-\zeta)p_{d,i}q,$$

such that operator i's market share is

$$\alpha_{d,i} \equiv \frac{1}{2} + \sigma_d[w_{d,i} - w_{d,j}] \text{ with } \sigma_d \equiv \frac{1}{2t_d}.$$

We assume $U_d(q)$ such that

$$v_d'(p_{d,i}) = -q.$$

Then, the first-order condition to (14) with respect to $p_{d,i}$ yields

$$p_{d,i} = c_{d,i} - (1-\alpha_{u,i})a - \alpha_{u,i}(p_{u,i} - c_{u,i})$$

or, in a symmetric equilibrium,

$$p_{d,i} = c_{d,i} - \frac{1}{2}a - \frac{1}{2}(p_{u,i} - c_{u,i}).$$

Hence, the networks' optimal downstream usage fee equals perceived marginal cost. Downstream market share is unaffected by it. However, the symmetric equilibrium subscriber fee determines the size of the downstream user base. It is given by

$$P_{d,i} = -\frac{d\pi_i}{d\alpha_{d,i}} + \frac{1}{2\sigma_d}$$

and therefore equal to the net marginal cost of adding a subscriber to the downstream network plus the Hotelling markup.

Each unit loss of downstream market share implies a profit loss of

$$\frac{d\pi_i}{d\alpha_{d,i}} = (p_d - c_d)q(p_u + \zeta p_d) - f_d + P_d$$

which is per-customer downstream profit when the two networks charge identical prices.

5.4 Simulation results and discussion

Our main goal is to derive optimal pricing structures in liberalized postal markets, where potentially all involved parties (senders, receivers, operators) can exert their bargaining power. Senders have the choice over competing operators; receivers can exclusively attribute a postal operator as their delivery partner of choice; and operators can establish a consumer base on one side of the market and sell it to the other one.

A calibration of the model enables us to numerically compute the operators' optimal pricing strategies as a function of the reciprocal interconnection rate. We calibrate the model to correspond roughly to the size and the characteristics of the Swiss letter market. The number of receivers is equal to 4m households and businesses. The current volume of addressed letters is 2.8bn at an average price of CHF 0.75 with price elasticity $\eta = 0.27$[70]. Utility parameter β is calibrated to 650 to represent the Swiss letter market with approximately 700 letters per year and receiver. Total cost is CHF 2bn.[71] With roughly 50% delivery cost of which 50% are fixed and a fraction of fixed cost of 30% in collection and processing, we calibrate f_u, c_u, f_d, and c_d accordingly. Moreover, we set $\sigma_u = \sigma_d = 0.2$.

---

[70] For a discussion of demand parameters cf. Trinkner and Grossmann (2006).
[71] For a discussion of the cost structure of the Swiss mail market, cf. Dietl et al. (2005) and Jaag (2006).

The following observations and results apply for the calibration as above. Other calibrations might yield different optimal pricing strategies. Note that Switzerland exhibits a very high postal scale[72]. Moreover, given the rough calibration and the stylized model, the results are only indicative.

Figure 20 displays the optimal pricing strategies depending on the exogenously set access price. We ran simulations with various values of ζ. Black lines are computed with $\zeta = 0.25$, dark grey lines with $\zeta = 0.5$ and light grey lines with $\zeta = 0.75$.

Figure 20: Optimal pricing structure depending on interconnection rate

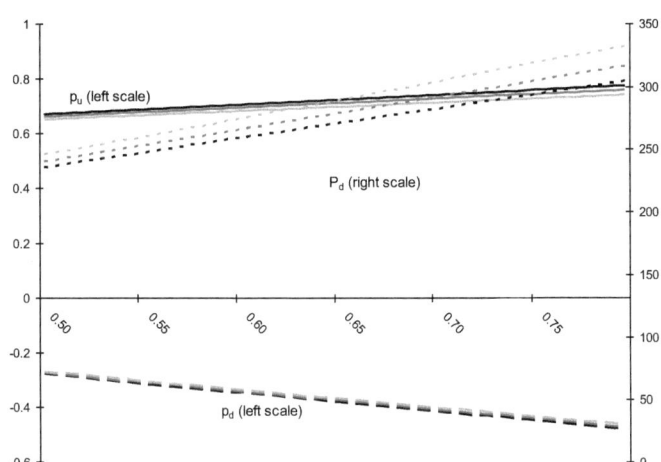

Observation 1 – Optimal pricing structure: The results replicate the pricing structure as observed in the completely liberalized postal market of New Zealand when market participants agreed on symmetric access prices to P.O. boxes. Given a similar regulatory regime, as set out in the model, we find an optimal pricing strategy in two-sided postal markets as follows: If the interconnection rate is about CHF 0.6, charge your key receivers a yearly delivery flat rate between CHF 250 and 300. In turn, for every mail piece you deliver now exclusively, you *pay* (not charge!) your client (the receiver) about CHF 0.3 per mail piece (i.e. p_d is negative). On the sender side, you charge about 0.7 per piece. In such a setting, given upstream and downstream variable costs and before considering fixed costs, net profits on end-to-end services are about break even, whereas

---

[72] See also PWC (2006).

upstream services incur a loss ($p_u - a < c_u$) and downstream products are profitable ($a + p_d > c_d$).

The results indicate that competition in two-sided postal markets forces operators to strongly cross-subsidize large receivers.

Figure 21 and Figure 22 show the effect of an increase of the interconnection rate on operators' profit per customer and mail volumes.

Figure 21: Postal operator profit per customer

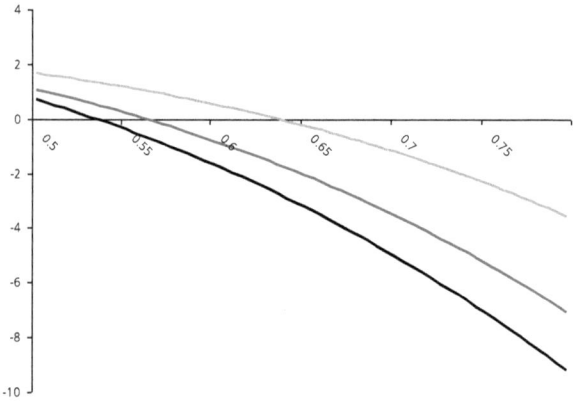

Figure 22: Mail Volumes

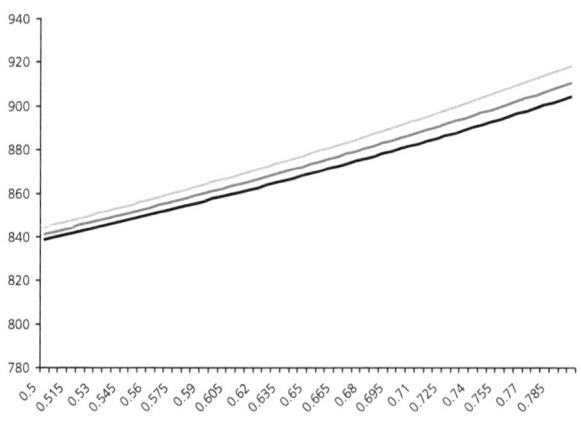

Observation 2 – Effect of interconnection charge: Increasing interconnection rates make the downstream business more attractive (higher earnings for downstream operators) and results in fiercer downstream competition. This forces the operators to give their subscribers higher per piece incentives (more negative p_d), which are funded by higher stamp prices. Partly, operators can recover higher incentives by higher subscriber fees, too. Note that the receivers' incentives grow faster than the stamp price due to the increased relative importance of downstream market shares (which are the basis for downstream profits). Interestingly, receivers' average price ($p_d + P_d/q$) becomes negative for high interconnection rates, i.e. they become subsidized and even make a profit by being connected to the postal network. Importantly, this redistribution comes at the cost of the networks, not at the cost of the senders, as the latter benefit from the receivers' better bargaining position by means of private rebalancing, which yields a lower price level $p_d + p_d$ and thus higher mail volumes q.

Thus, if we can exclude tacit collusion, high interconnection rates make the industry unattractive, as receivers are given a high bargaining position by means of regulation.

Observation 3 – Effect of private redistribution: A higher value of ζ enables senders and receivers better to offset pricing structures by means of private redistribution. Recapitulate that at the extreme ($\zeta = 1$) complete pass-through of per piece prices takes place such that mail volumes $q(p)$ depend just on the sum of the two variable prices $p = p_u + p_d$. Hence, the mail originating side includes total marginal postage into its calculations.

Since the downstream price p_d is negative, such redistribution leads to a participation of senders in downstream incentives, which decreases their perceived costs and thereby increases volumes (cf. Figure 22) and profits (cf. Figure 21). Put differently, if receivers not only are able to exert their market power towards the operators, but also towards the senders (lower value of ζ), we can expect negative demand effects and a significant drop of industry profits.

Hence, if receivers not only are able to exert their market power towards the operators, but also towards the senders, we can expect negative demand effects and a significant drop of industry profits.

5.5 Conclusions

Practical evidence from postal markets suggests that mail markets are two-sided. Hence, postal operators are platforms that enable communication and transactions between two parties – senders/mailers on one side, and receivers/recipients on the other. This two-sidedness raises two main issues, network effects and pricing.

Network effects are present in most two-sided markets, and most probably in postal markets too. We can expect the value of a postal network to increase the more customers are connected to it. We presume that the notion of ubiquitous access and delivery, which lies at the core of the universal service obligation, is to be seen in this context. We do not include network effects directly into our model (although indirect network effects between the upstream and downstream market are present) as we are primarily interested in the pricing implications of the two-sidedness of the postal market.

In terms of pricing, the two-sidedness makes things more complicated. Standard results of economic theory (related to one-sided markets) might fail in two-sided markets. Wright (2004) spells out "eight fallacies that arise from using one-sided logic in two-sided markets" and concludes that "the results may be very different from the normal marginal cost pricing familiar in one-sided markets". In our model, the interconnection of the two sides (upstream and downstream) of the mail market yields interesting pricing considerations, which are a challenge for pricing departments as well as for regulators and competition authorities. In posts, recipients traditionally have been served by monopoly platforms that charged the senders and served receivers free of charge. This still holds true in virtually any industrialized country. For example, Swiss recipients get home delivery and P.O. boxes free of charge, the latter having the advantage of early morning delivery.

How do things change in liberalized two-sided mail markets? Will receivers remain subsidized? Our results indicate that in liberalized markets at least key receivers will be subsidized even stronger at the cost of the postal industry. Depending on P.O. box regulations, the optimal strategy of postal operators towards receivers will be to offer them a costly P.O. box while paying them money for every mail piece delivered to this P.O. box. Thereby, large receivers will succeed in capitalizing on their address. Such a pricing would have harmful effects on overall mail volumes unless senders participate accordingly (unlikely for the case of direct mail). We conclude that it is very risky for postal operators to introduce receivers' pricing or incentives. This result may not hold for value added services. The results raise the more general question of who should pay for postal services from a welfare point of view. Jaag (2007) proposes a model framework to address such issues.

The current common regulatory view states that P.O. boxes are monopolistic bottlenecks with a respective need of access regulation. This is somewhat astonishing as there are no sunk costs related to P.O. box provision (cf. Table 6). Our two-sided model suggests that we can expect competition for P.O. boxes as observed in New Zealand[73] and that operators have a common interest for low access prices. Hence, in terms of P.O. box regulations, our results contradict the common view. We leave it for further research to assess whether this holds also true for models with asymmetric equilibria. However, as Panzar (2006) points out, the two-sidedness of the postal market makes access regulation to P.O. boxes a rather complex task and cost based pricing rules rather inappropriate.

---

[73] Nee Zealand Post currently holds about 90% market share in P.O. box provision.

6. Concluding Remarks

In this book we asked whether Switzerland should open its letters market completely to competition. From an economic point of view this question comes down to the aim of maximizing the long run overall welfare in Switzerland subject to certain constraints. Such constraints could be the set of politically feasible regulations, social objectives that arise from market failures, or ensuring the provision of universal postal services.

6.1 Two conflicting concepts: Universal Service and Free Market

Universal service is a major concern in the postal market[74] and faces great attention throughout the liberalization processes in Europe and elsewhere. Thereby, some core elements of the so called universal service obligation (USO) such as affordable and uniform prices directly conflict with the notion of pure competition where the "invisible hand", the free pricing mechanism, ensures that supply and demand balance. Hence, free competition (prices = marginal costs) and universal service obligations (prices = uniform) are in a natural conflict as the former can only work at its best if prices are determined in the market and not in a political process. A similar argument can be made in terms of scope and quality of universal services.

Hence, one first challenge for policy makers is to ensure the fulfillment of USO while providing a level playing field that offers a prosperous base for effective and welfare improving competition with consumers' choice over a great variety of fairly priced products based on an efficient service provision by postal operators. As long as the USO constraints are economically binding (i.e. the cost of the USO[75] is positive), the market will not provide the universal services as requested and thus market interventions (regulations) become necessary. In principle, two concepts are on the table.

---

[74] Positive externalities associated to universal postal services offer an economic interpretation of the broad political response to any change related to USO. Cf. Dietl and Trinkner (2008) for a discussion of the economic importance of universal postal services.

[75] See Cremer et al. (2000), Panzar (2001), Oxera (2006), Dietl et al. (2007) or Jaag et al. (2009) for guidance on how to calculate the Cost of USO. Note that this "Cost of the Universal Service Obligation" matters for determining the financing needs whereas the "Cost of the Universal Service" or the "Profit of the USO provider" do not provide any guidance.

Firstly, one might impose USO constraints on any operator. This solution is less demanding in terms of regulation but might be inefficient[76] or raise barriers to entry which conflicts the aim of market opening. Secondly, one might designate just one operator who has to comply with USO constraints (ex ante or by public procurement). Ensuring a level playing field involves an adequate compensation of the designated universal service provider either through external funds such as government subsidies or through a compensation fund mechanism as foreseen in the current Swiss postal law where operators other than the universal service provider contribute according to their turnover[77].

Our calculations show that such a compensation fund – given the current USO of Switzerland – only succeeds if the licensing fees are set at levels that almost entirely prevent entry. Hence, government subsidies might be the only stable solution allowing for competition with operators other than the incumbent. However, such subsidies raise the floor for inefficient entries (by sustaining the incumbent's higher mark ups in low cost areas) that moreover increase the financing need for providing the USO.

In light of these considerations, the only suitable solution might be to reduce the USO itself and to align it as much as possible with the market. Prominent ambassadors of this standpoint are Crew and Kleindorfer (2006b, p. 13): "… under entry the USO will have to decrease if inefficient subsidies and compensation funds are to be avoided. We also showed that there is a trade-off between USO and the level of competitiveness [of the USP] for business customers." Into the same direction points the impact assessment of PWC on behalf of the European Commission (PWC 2006a, p. 23) which recommends to "adapt the USO to market conditions", that is:

> "We use the term 'adapting the USO to market conditions' to mean generally achieving a better alignment of price, cost and value for USO services. This might include, for example, using postal employees to provide services in rural areas as part of their routes rather than at fixed counters, increased use of franchised operations, increasing the stamp price, and eliminating uniformity requirements on business-originated mail. Adapting the USO could also mean changing the constraints on accessibility for counters and collection services as populations and demand for postal services change over time."

We conclude that the natural conflict between competition and USO is not to be neglected in the postal sector. Crew and Kleindorfer (2006b, p. 13) summarize: "The more

---

[76] Consider a case as Switzerland where the post office network is part of the USO. Such a system would yield – if market entries ever occurred – to far too many post offices.

[77] "Pay or play" mechanisms somehow mix the two systems. Operators can avoid to "paying" into the compensation fund by "playing", i.e. providing the USO too. Note that tendering is a method to allocate the USO, not a financing mechanism by itself. See Jaag and Trinkner (2008b) for a discussion on tendering USO in liberalized markets.

stringent is the competition from entrants, the higher the burden of the USO [...], and the lower the scope of the welfare-optimal level of USO." This trade-off between USO and competition is of particular importance in Switzerland where the market is attractive to new entrants and the level of USO is comparably high[78]. PWC (2006b) illustrates the trade-off and gives guidance on the deficit one has to expect for the universal service provider after a full market opening keeping USO constraints unchanged. We conclude with a statement by Crew and Kleindorfer (2006a p. 21): "All of this raises the broader question of whether the USO has had its day."

6.2 Impact of a Full Market Opening on Welfare

The previous remarks indicate the difficulties in finding a suitable financing instrument for the USO that enables "workable" competition at the same time. Things get even more complex if one wants to consider the impact on overall welfare too.

Our results in Chapter 4 indicate that a full market opening yields only welfare improvements if accompanied with a price freeze for the incumbent and massive subsidies to compensate its resulting burden[79]. In all other scenarios, our model predicts a loss of overall welfare which is in line with many studies undertaken on the subject. Hence the trade-off between competition and universal service reveals itself as a trade-off between universal service obligations on the one hand and the universal service provider's financial burden and a respective need for subsidies on the other. For example, the more restrictions are imposed on the incumbent's pricing flexibility the worse becomes the financial situation of the incumbent.

In contrast to our assessment of the European way to foster competition in the mail industry, our analysis yields better results for the US regulations which base on a rigid letters monopoly but allow for upstream innovation and competition. In line with the literature, we predict higher welfare and much better USP stability than various ways of end-to-end competition.

We conclude that Switzerland should be very cautious when copying European plans of end-to-end competition. We believe caution is especially indicated if our estimation results of high economies of scale and density in delivery truly reflect the industry. Our calculations predict that complete letter market liberalization will lead to higher prices, to increased price differentiation between regions and customers (in favor of business customers and cities), and to an erosion of universal services due to

---

[78] See for example Finger (2007), PostReg (2006) or PWC (2006b).
[79] PWC (2006b) provides similar results.

continuous financial pressure on the universal service provider. These problems will even tighten if a full market opening was combined with an access regime under which competitors could use the incumbent's delivery network when and where needed.

Our model cannot cope with some dynamic advantages of competition. For example, we did not model dynamic efficiency gains of Swiss Post differently under end-to-end competition compared to monopoly scenarios. If one believes those efficiency potentials to be large, then end-to-end competition could still be a desirable solution. However, postal services already face increasing indirect competition through digital means of written communication. Despite growing written communication markets, overall mail volumes are shrinking in most highly developed countries including Switzerland. This rapidly evolving "e-competition" threatens the postal services in a similar way as end-to-end competition does. This raises competitive pressure with a respective need for efficiency and innovation which is independent of liberalization. Thereby, it is crucial that the industry finds ways to successfully position itself in this broader market for communications and advertisement where prices for digital deliveries are marginal. Should postal operators primarily focus on market positioning against each other by climbing down the quality latter, the industry might find itself in a difficult situation. Fortunately, first success stories from overseas are on the table.

In sum one might ask where the overall welfare gains of a full market opening should stem from. If solid pressure for cost reductions is present independently of liberalization[80], if the relative effect on innovation is indeed limited[81], if a duplication of networks is inevitable and thus economies of scale and density are less exploited, if one has to expect an increase at least in retail prices, and if postal markets are two-sided, ours and many others' results might give adequate guidance of what Switzerland can expect from liberalizing its mail market completely: Welfare gains will be limited, and universal service obligations at risk.

---

[80] Be it through e-substitution or modern incentive regulations.
[81] Andersson (2006): "The Swedish market is not significantly more innovative than other modern postal markets". See Dietl et al. (2006) for the impact of end-to-end competition on incentives for innovation.

Abbreviations

BtoC	Business to consumer
Cf.	Confer
CHF	Swiss Francs
CPI	Consumer price index
e.g.	exempli gratia – for example
ECPR	Efficient component pricing rule
ED	Economies of density
ES	Economies of scale
ESS	Economies of scale
EU	European Union
FMO	Full market opening
FOC	First order condition
FTE	Full time equivalent
GDP	Gross domestic product
i.e.	id est – that is
MH	Multiplicative Heteroscedastic
OLS	Ordinary least squares
P.O.	Post office
PostReg	Postal regulatory authority of Switzerland
PRC	Postal Regulatory Commission
PTT	Post-, Telefon- und Telegrafenbetriebe
RC	Regulated competition
RM	Regulated monopoly
seco	State Secretariat for Economic Affairs
SM1	Substitution Model 1
SM2	Substitution Model 2
SMS	Short Message Service
TM	Traditional Model
TV	Television
UC	Unregulated competition

UK	United Kingdom
UM	Unregulated monopoly
UPU	Universal Postal Union
US	United States
USO	Universal service obligation
USP	Universal service provider
USPS	United States Postal Service
UVEK	Federal Department of the Environment, Transport, Energy and Communications
VAT	Value added tax
VEC	Vector error correction model
WLS	Weighted least squares
WS	Worksharing

List of Tables

Table 1: Overview of quarterly data set 12
Table 2: Unrestricted cointegration rank test 16
Table 3: Estimation results (Dependent variable: overall mail volume) 17
Table 4: Distribution of total costs 26
Table 5: Economies of scope, scale and density 33
Table 6: Contestability in dependence of cost characteristics 37
Table 7: Major demand characteristics 47
Table 8: Major cost characteristics 48
Table 9: Results monopoly cases 50
Table 10: Results End-to-End Competition 52
Table 11: Results Worksharing and Price Cap Competition 59
Table 12: Overview of pricing structures in two-sided markets 68

List of Figures

Figure 1: Historical development of addressed mail items in Switzerland 9
Figure 2: Quarterly mail demand (seasonally adjusted) 10
Figure 3: Residuals of static OLS regression, R^2=97%, DW=0.57 10
Figure 4: Recursive estimates yield increasing price elasticity 14
Figure 5: Demand shock after a 10% price increase 18
Figure 6: Exogenous (left) and endogenous (right) predictions TM 20
Figure 7: Exogenous (left) and endogenous (right) predictions SM1 21
Figure 8: Exogenous (left) and endogenous (right) predictions SM2 21
Figure 9: E-Substitution as a loss of market share in platform competition 23
Figure 10: The postal value chain 25
Figure 11: Swiss Post's organization of mail delivery as of 2004 30
Figure 12: Overview over various liberalization and regulatory policies 40
Figure 13: Model outline 42
Figure 14: Impact of the licensing rate on welfare and profits 54
Figure 15: EU market opening compared to US worksharing 56
Figure 16: Stylized worksharing model 57
Figure 17: Development of overall mail volumes in selected high-volume countries 60
Figure 18: Illustration of a possible two-part tariff in the postal sector 65
Figure 19: Model outline 71
Figure 20: Optimal pricing structure depending on interconnection rate 77
Figure 21: Postal operator profit per customer 78
Figure 22: Mail Volumes 78

References

Andersson, Peter. 2006. *The Liberalisation of Postal Services in Sweden – Goals, Results, and Lessons for Other Countries*. Study on behalf of seco.

Armstrong, Mark. 2001. *Access Pricing, Bypass and Universal Service*. American Economic Review, Papers and Proceedings 91(2): 297-301.

Armstrong, Mark. 2006a. *Competition in Two-Sided Markets*. RAND Journal of Economics. Vol. 37, No. 3, pp. 668–691.

Armstrong, Mark. 2006b. *Access pricing, bypass and universal service in post*. MPRA Paper No. 62. University Library of Munich, Germany. Presented at the 3rd conference on Regulation, competition and universal service in the postal sector.

Baumol, W. J. 1977. *On the Proper Cost Test for Natural Monopolies in a Multiproduct Industry*, American Economic Review, 67, 809-822.

Baumol, W. J., J. C. Panzar and R. D. Willig. 1982. *Contestable Markets and the Theory of Industry Structure*, Hartcourt Brace Jovanovich, Inc.

Billette de Villemeur, Etienne Billette, Helmuth Cremer, Bernard Roy and Joëlle Toledano. 2004a. "Worksharing, pricing and competition in the postal sector." In *Regulatory and Economic Changes in the Postal and Delivery Sector*, edited by M. A. Crew and P. R. Kleindorfer, Boston: Kluwer Academic Publishers, 139—162.

Billette de Villemeur, Etienne Billette, Helmuth Cremer, Bernard Roy and Joëlle Toledano. 2004b. "Access and (Non-) Uniform Pricing in the Postal Sector" In *Competitive Transformation of The Postal and Delivery Sector*, edited by Michael A. Crew and Paul R. Kleindorfer. Boston, MA: Kluwer Academic Publishers.

Bradley, Michael D. and Jeff Colvin. 1995. "An Econometric Model of Postal Delivery." In *Commercialization of Postal and Delivery Services*, edited by Michael A. Crew and Paul R. Kleindorfer. Boston, MA: Kluwer Academic Publishers. 137-53.

Bundesnetzagentur. 2006. *Neunte Marktuntersuchung für den Bereich der lizenzpflichtigen Postdienstleistungen*. Bundesnetzagentur für Elektrizität, Gas, Telekommunikation, Post, und Eisenbahnen. Mainz.

Bundesrat. 2002. *Gesamtschau zur weiteren Entwicklung des Postwesens in der Schweiz – Bericht des Bundesrates und Botschaft über die Änderung des Postorganisationsgesetzes vom 5. 2002*.

Buser, Martin, Christian Jaag and Urs Trinkner. 2008. "Economics of Post Office Networks: Strategic Issues and the Impact on Mail Demand". In *Handbook of Global Postal Reform*, edited by M. A. Crew, P. R. Kleindorfer, and J. Campbell. Cheltenham, UK, Edward Elgar, pp. 80-97.

Campell, James I. 2004. *History of Universal Service in the United States*. Presented at the 12th Conference on Postal and Delivery Economics in Cork.

Cazalda, Juan. 2006. *Worksharing and access discounts in the postal sector with asymmetric information*, Journal of Regulatory Economics. Springer, Volume 29/1, 69 — 102.

Cazals, C., J.-P. Florens and B. Roy. 2001. "An Analysis of Some Specific Cost Drivers in the Delivery Activity." In *Future Directions in Postal Reform*, edited by M.A. Crew and P.R. Kleindorfer, Boston, MA: Kluwer Academic Publishers.

Cazals, C., J.-P. Florens and S. Soteri. 2005. "Delivery Costs for Postal Services in the UK: Some Results on Scale Economies with Panel Data." In *Regulatory and Economic Challenges in the Postal and Delivery Sector*, edited by M.A. Crew and P.R. Kleindorfer. Boston, MA: Kluwer Academic Publishers.

Cazals, Catherine and Jean-Pierre Florens. 2002. "Econometrics of Mail Demand" In *Postal and Delivery Services: Delivering on Competition*, edited by Michael A. Crew and Paul R. Kleindorfer. Boston, MA: Kluwer Academic Publishers.

Cohen, Robert H. and E.H. Chu. 1997. "A Measure of Scale Economies for Postal Systems." In *Managing Change in the Postal and Delivery Industries*, edited by M.A. Crew and P.R. Kleindorfer. Boston: Kluwer Academic Publishers.

Cohen, Robert H., Matthew Robinson, Renee Sheehy, Tom Sharkey, John Waller and Spyros Xenakis. 2005. *The conflict about preserving samall rural post offices: difference in the distribution of pharmacies and post offices*. Presented at the 9th Königswinter Seminar. Wik.

Cohen, Robert H., William W. Ferguson, John D. Waller and Spyros S. Xenakis. 2002. "The Impact of Using Worksharing to Liberalize a Postal Market." In *Liberalisation of Postal Markets*, edited by Gabriele Kulenkampff and Hilke Smit. Rheinbreitbach.

Cremer, H., A. Grimaud and J.-J. Laffont. 2000. "The Cost of Universal Service in the Postal Sector." In *Current Directions in Postal Reform*, edited by M. A. Crew and P R. Kleindorfer, Boston: Kluwer Academic Publishers, pp. 47-68.

Crew, Michael A. and Paul R. Kleindorfer. 1991. "Rowland Hill's Contribution as an Economist." In *Competition and Innovation in Postal Services*, edited by M.A. Crew and P.R. Kleindorfer. Boston: Kluwer Academic Publishers.

Crew, Michael A. and Paul R. Kleindorfer. 2002. "Balancing Access and the Universal Service Obligation." In *Postal and Delivery Services: Delivering on Competition*, edited by M.A. Crew and P.R. Kleindorfer. Boston, MA: Kluwer Academic Publishers.

Crew, Michael A. and Paul R. Kleindorfer. 2002. "Putty-Putty, Putty-Clay or Humpty-Dumpty? Universal Service Under Entry." In *Postal and Delivery Services: Pricing, Productivity, Regulation and Strategy*, edited by Michael A. Crew and Paul R. Kleindorfer. Boston, MA: Kluwer Academic Publishers.

Crew, Michael A. and Paul R. Kleindorfer. 2004. "Access and the USO for Letters and Parcels": In *Competitive Transformation of the Postal and Delivery Sector*, edited by Michael A. Crew and Paul R. Kleindorfer. Boston, MA: Kluwer Academic Publishers.

Crew, Michael A. and Paul R. Kleindorfer. 2006a. "The Welfare Effects of Entry and Strategies for Maintaining the USO in the Postal Sector." In *Progress Toward Liberalization of the Postal and Delivery Sector*, edited by M.A. Crew and P.R. Kleindorfer. New York: Springer Science+Business Media, Inc.

Crew, Michael A. and Paul R. Kleindorfer. 2006b. "Approaches to the USO unter Entry". In *Liberalization of the Postal and Delivery Sector*, edited by M. A. Crew and P. R. Kleindorfer. Edward Elgar.

De Donder P., H. Cremer and F. Rodriguez. 2004. "Access Pricing in the Postal Sector: Results from a Model with Bypass and Customer Direct Access", in *Regulatory and Economics Changes in the Postal and Delivery Sector*, edited by M.A. Crew and P.R. Kleindorfer, Boston: Kluwer Academic Publishers, 163-188.

De Donder, Philippe, Helmuth Cremer and Frank Rodriguez. 2004. "Access Pricing and Uniform Tariff in the Postal Sector." In *Competitive Transformation of the Postal and Delivery Sector*, edited by Michael A. Crew and Paul R. Kleindorfer. Boston, MA: Kluwer Academic Publishers.

De Donder, Philippe, Helmuth Cremer, Jean-Pierre Florens, André Grimaud and Frank Rodriguez. 2001. "Uniform Pricing and Postal Market Liberalization." In *Future Directions in Postal Reform*, edited by M. A. Crew and Paul R. Kleindorfer. Boston, MA: Kluwer Academic Publishers.

De Donder, Philippe, Helmuth Cremer, Paul Dudley and Frank Rodriguez. 2006. "A Welfare Analysis of Price Controls with End-to-End Mail and Access Services." In *Liberalization of the Postal and Delivery Sector*, edited by M. A. Crew and P. R. Kleindorfer. Edward Elgar.

De Donder, Philippe. 2006. *Access Pricing in the Postal Sector: Theory and Simulations*. Review of Industrial Organization, 2006, vol. 28, issue 3, pages 307-326.

Dietl, Helmut M. and Peter Waller. 2002. "Competing with Mr. Postman: Business Strategies, Industry Structure, and Competitive Prices in Liberalized Letter Markets." In *Schmalenbach Business Review*, Vol. 54, pp 148 – 170, zfbf, Verlagsgruppe Handelsblatt.

Dietl, Helmut M. and Urs Trinkner. 2008. *Developing the Universal Service in Low Volume Countries – an Economic Perspective*. Working Paper. University of Zurich. Spanish Version Forthcoming 2009.

Dietl, Helmut M., Andreas Grütter and Martin Lutzenberger. 2007. *Erhebung der Kosten für die Grundversorgung – Vor- und Nachteile der Methoden*. Die Volkswirtschaft, published by seco.

Dietl, Helmut M., Urs Trinkner and Reto Bleisch. 2005. "Liberalization and Regulation of the Swiss Letter Market." In *Regulatory and Economic Challenges in the Postal and Delivery Sector*, edited by M.A. Crew and P.R. Kleindorfer. Boston, MA: Kluwer Academic Publishers.

Dietl, Helmut. M., Andreas Grütter and Martin Lutzerberger. 2006. *Deregulation of Letter Markets and its Impact on Process and Product Innovation*, presented at the 4th Postal Conference "Regulation, Competition and Universal Service in the Postal Sector", IDEI, Toulouse.

Doyle, C. and J.C. Smith. 1998. *Market structure in mobile telecoms: qualified indirect access and the receiver pays principle*. Information Economics and Policy 10: 471-488.

Ecorys. 2005. *Development of Competition in the European Postal Sector*. Study on behalf of the European Commission.

Elsenbast, W. 1996. *Die Infrastrukturverpflichtung im Postbereich aus Nutzersicht*. Diskussionbeitrag Nr. 162, WIK, Bad Honnef.

European Commission Proposal for a Directive of the European Parliament and of the Council amending Directive 97/67/EC concerning the full accomplishment of the internal market of Community postal services COM. 2006. 594 final.

Farsi, Mehdi, Massimo Filippini and Urs Trinkner. 2006. "*Economies of scale, density and scope in Swiss Post's Mail Delivery*." In Liberalization of the Postal and Delivery Sector, edited by M. A. Crew and P. R. Kleindorfer. Edward Elgar.

Felisberto, Catia, Matthias Finger, Beat Friedl, Daniel Krahenbuhl and Urs Trinkner. 2006. "Pricing the Last Mile in the Postal Sector." In *Progress Toward Liberalization of the Postal and Delivery Sector*, edited by M.A. Crew and P.R. Kleindorfer. New York: Springer Science+Business Media, Inc.

Filippini, M. and M. Zola. 2005. *Economies of scale and cost efficiency in the postal services: empirical evidence from Switzerland*. Applied Economics Letters, 12, 437-441.

Finger, Matthias. 2004. *Fallstudie Schweizer Post*, mimeo, EPFL Lausanne.

Finger, Matthias. 2007. *Umfang und Finanzierungsmöglichkeiten des postalischen Universaldienstes bei vollständiger Marktöffnung.* Die Volkswirtschaft, published by seco.

Florens, Jean Pierre, Sarah Marcy and Joelle Toledano. 2002. "Mail Demand in the Long and Short Term." In *Postal and Delivery Services: Pricing, Productivity, Regulation and Strategy*, edited by Michael A. Crew and Paul R. Kleindorfer. Boston, MA: Kluwer Academic Publishers.

Friedli, Beat, Christian Jaag, Daniel Krähenbühl, Ole Bach Nielsen, Søren Michael Pihl and Urs Trinkner. 2006. "Consumer Preferences and Last Mile Pricing in the Postal Sector." In *Liberalization of the Postal and Delivery Sector*, edited by M.A. Crew and P.R. Kleindorfer. Cheltenham, UK and Lyme, US: Edward Elgar.

Gautier, Axel. 2006. "Dynamics of Downstream Entry in Postal Markets" In *Liberalization of the Postal and Delivery Sector*, edited by M. A. Crew and P. R. Kleindorfer. Edward Elgar.

Gori, S., E. Piccinijn, S. Romito and G. Scarfiglieri. 2006. "On the Use of Cost Functions in the Assessment of the Impact of Liberalization on Postal Universal Service Burden: Restricted versus Flexible Specifications." In *Progress toward liberalization of the postal and delivery sector*, edited by M.A. Crew and P.R. Kleindorfer, Springer.

Hamilton, J.D. 1994. *Time Series Analysis*. Princeton, NJ: Princeton University Press.

Harding, Matthew C. 2004. *Mail Demand Models*. Paper presented at the XIII International Conference on Postal and Delivery Economics, Antwerp, June 4-7, 2005.

Hemmeon, J.C. 1912. *The History of the British Post Office*. London, Henry Frowde.

Hermalin, B.E. and M.L. Katz. 2004: *"Sender or Receiver: who should pay to exchange an electronic message?"* Rand Journal of Economics 35(3): 423-447.

Hill, R. and Hill, G.B. 1880: *The Life of Sir Rowland Hill*. London: Thos. De La Rue & Co.

Jaag, Christian and Urs Trinkner. 2007. *Schwedische Postmarktöffnung - ein Modell für die Schweiz?* Die Volkswirtschaft, published by seco.

Jaag, Christian and Urs Trinkner. 2008a. "Pricing in competitive two-sided mail markets." In *Competition and Regulation in the Postal and Delivery Sector*, edited by M. A. Crew and P. R. Kleindorfer. Cheltenham, UK and Northampton, MA, USA: Edward Elgar, pp. 136 - 149.

Jaag, Christian and Urs Trinkner. 2008b. *Tendering Universal Service Obligations in Liberalized Markets: An Outline of Thought*. Working Paper. Presented in Lausanne at the 2nd GPREN conference.

Jaag, Christian, Martin Koller and Urs Trinkner. Forthcoming 2009. "Calculating the Cost of the USO - The Need for a Global Approach". In *Progress in the Competitive Agenda in the Postal and Delivery Sector*, edited by M. A. Crew and P. R. Kleindorfer. Cheltenham, UK, Edward Elgar.

Jaag, Christian. 2006. *"Liberalization of the Swiss Letter market and the Viability of Universal Service Obligations"*, mimeo, Swiss Post.

Jaag, Christian. 2007. *"Who should pay for postal services? Tax payers vs. Senders vs. Receivers."* Presentation held at the 1st GPREN Postal Research Conference.

Jeon, D.S., J.J. Laffont and J. Tirole. 2004. *"On the Receiver Pays Principle."* Rand Journal of Economics 35(1): 85-110.

Kim, J.Y. and Y. Lim. 2000. *"An Economic Analysis of the Receiver Pays Principle."* Information Economics and Policy 13: 231-260.

Knieps, Günter. 2002. "Does the system of letter conveyance constitute a bottleneck resource?" In *Contestability and Barriers to Entry in Postal Markets*, edited by Gabriele Kuhlenkampff und Antonia Niederprüm, published in 2006 by WIK, Rheinbreitbach, p. 9 – 22.

Knieps, Günter. 2005. *Wettbewerbsökonomie*. Dritte überarbeitete Auflage. Springer, Berlin

Kruse, Jörn and Andreas Liebe. 2005. *Netzzugang und Wettbewerb bei Briefdiensten*. Studie im Auftrag des Bundesverbandes Internationaler Express- und Kurierdienste (BIEK).

Laffont, Jean-Jacques, Patrick Rey and Jean Tirole. 1998. *"Network Competition: I. Overview and Nondiscriminatory Pricing."* RAND Journal of Economics 29(1): pp.1-37.

Mizutani, F. and S. Uranishi. 2003. *The Post Office vs. Parcel delivery Companies: Competition Effects on Costs and Productivity*. Journal of Regulatory Economics, 23 (3): 299-319.

Nader, Fouad H. 2004. *Mail Trends*. Available at http://www.postinsight.pb.com.

Nankervis, John and Frank Rodriguez. 1995. "Aggregate Letter Traffic Demand in the United Kingdom and the Economy." In *Commercialization of Postal and Delivery Services*, edited by Michael A. Crew and Paul R. Kleindorfer. Boston, MA: Kluwer Academic Publishers.

Nankervis, John, Isabelle Carslake and Frank Rodriguez. 1999. "How Important Have Price and Quality of Service Been to Mail Volume Growth?" In *Emerging Competition in Postal and Delivery Services*, edited by Michael A. Crew and Paul R. Kleindorfer. Boston, MA: Kluwer Academic Publishers.

Nankervis, John, Sophie Richard, Soterios Soteri and Frank Rodriguez. 2002. "Disaggregated Letter Traffic Demand in the UK." In *Postal and Delivery Services: Pricing, Productivity, Regulation and Strategy*, edited by Michael A. Crew and Paul R. Kleindorfer. Boston, MA: Kluwer Academic Publishers.

NERA. 2004. *Economics of Postal Services: Final Report*, A report to the European Commission, NERA Economic Consulting, London.

Nikali, Heikki. 1997. "Demand Models for Letter Mail and Its Substitutes: Results from Finland." In *Managing Change in the Postal and Delivery Industries*, edited by Michael A. Crew and Paul R. Kleindorfer. Boston, MA: Kluwer Academic Publishers.

Nikali, Heikki. 1998. *The Substitution of Letter Mail in Targeted Communication*. Helsinki: Finland Post Ltd, Quality and Business Development. Research Publications 27/1998. (May).

Owen, B. and R. Willig. 1981. "Economics and postal pricing". In *The Future of the Postal Service*, edited by J. Fleishman. Aspen: The Aspen Institute.

Oxera. 2007. *Funding Universal Service Obligations in the Postal Sector*. Study on behalf of nine European Postal Operators.

Panzar, John C. 2001. "Funding Universal Service Obligations: The Costs of Liberalization." In *Future Directions in Postal Reform*, edited by Michael A. Crew and Paul R. Kleindorfer. Boston, MA: Kluwer Academic Publishers.

Panzar, John C. 2002a. "Reconciling competition, downstream access and universal service and universal service in postal markets", in *Postal and Delivery Services: Delivering on Competition*, edited by M. A. Crew and P. R. Kleindorfer, Boston: Kluwer Academic Publishers, 93—115.

Panzar, John C. 2002b. "Are postal markets contestable?" In *Contestability and Barriers to Entry in Postal Markets*, edited by Gabriele Kuhlenkampff und Antonia Niederprüm, published in 2006 by WIK, Rheinbreitbach, p. 1 – 8.

Panzar, John C. 2004. *The Economic Effects of Combining Liberalization and Unbundling Policies in Postal Markets*. mimeo Northwestern University and University of Auckland. Presented at the Third Conference on Regulation, Competition and Universal Service in the Postal Sector, Toulouse.

Panzar, John C. 2006. *"PO Box Access: Competition Issues in a Two-Sided Postal Market."* Presentation held in Toulouse at the 4th IDEI/La Poste Conference on Regulation, Competition and Universal Service in the Postal Sector.

Pimenta, Alberto A. and Patricia M. Ferreira. 1999. "Demand for Letters in Portugal." In *Emerging Competition in Postal and Delivery Services*, edited by Michael A. Crew and Paul R. Kleindorfer. Boston, MA: Kluwer Academic Publishers.

Plaut Economics & Frontier Economics. 2007. *Auswirkungen Postmarktliberalisierung 2011*. Study on behalf of UVEK.

Postal Solutions. 2003. *What is driving direct mail?*

PostReg. 2005. *PostReg Tätigkeitsbericht 2004*.

PostReg. 2006. *PostReg Tätigkeitsbericht 2005*.

PostReg. 2007. *PostReg Tätigkeitsbericht 2006*.

PricewaterhouseCoppers. 2006. "*Evaluating the Impact of a Full Market Opening on Swiss Post.*" Study commissioned by Swiss Post.

PWC. 2006a. *The Impact on Universal Service of the Full Market Accomplishment of the Postal Internal Market in 2009*. Study on behalf of European Commission.

PWC. 2006b. *Evaluating the Impact of a Full Market Opening on Swiss Post*. Study on behalf of Swiss Post.

RegTP. 2005. *Achte Marktuntersuchung für den Bereich der lizenzpflichtigen Postdienstleistungen*.

Rochet, Jean-Charles and Jean Tirole. 2003. "*Platform Competition in Two-Sided Markets.*" Journal of the European Economic Association. 1: pp. 990-1029.

Rochet, Jean-Charles and Jean Tirole. 2005. "*Two-sided markets: A progress Report.*" Mimeo, IDEI University of Toulouse.

Schwarz-Schilling, C. 2001. *Pricing Schemes in Liberalized Postal Markets*. Presented at the Second Conference on "Competition and Universal Service in the Postal Sector," Toulouse, December 6-7.

seco. 2005. *Bericht zur Dienstleistungsliberalisierung in der Schweiz im Vergleich zur EU*.

Smith, Adam. 1776. *An Inquiry into the Nature and Causes of the Wealth of Nations*, reprinted 1976 in W.B. Todd (ed.), Glasgow Edition of the Works and Correspondence of Adam Smith, vol. I, Oxford: Oxford University Press.

Trinkner, Urs and Martin Grossmann. 2006. "Forecasting Swiss Mail Demand." In *Progress Toward Liberalization of the Postal and Delivery Sector*, edited by M.A. Crew and P.R. Kleindorfer. New York: Springer Science+Business Media, Inc.

Trinkner, Urs. 2008. *Neue Postrichtlinie: Spielräume der Mitgliedsstaaten bei der Umsetzung, Konsequenzen für den Binnenmarkt und Folgen für die Schweizer Postpolitik*. M.B.L. Thesis at the University of St. Gallen, forthcoming in "Aktuelle Entwicklungen des Europäischen und Internationalen Wirtschaftsrechts", Verlag Helbing und Lichtenhahn.

Vaterlaus, Stephan and Patrick Zenhäusern. 2007. *Postmarkt Schweiz: Folgerungen aus dem schwedischen Beispiel und der ökonomischen Theorie*. Die Volkswirtschaft, published by seco.

Vaterlaus, Stephan, Heike Worm, Jörg Wild and Harald Telser. 2003. *Liberalisierung und Performance in Netzsektoren*. Studie im Auftrag des Staatssekretariats für Wirtschaft, Strukturberichterstattung Nr. 22.

Wada, T., C. Tsunoda and J. Nemoto. 1997. *Empirical Analysis of Economies of Scale, Economies of Scope, and Cost subadditivity in japanese Mail Service*. IPTP paper series 1997-08.

Waller, Peter. 2001. *Wettbewerbsstrategie in liberalisierten Briefmärkten*. Lohmar/Köln (Eul), 2002.

Wik-Consult. 2004. *Main developments Main Developments in the European Postal Sector*. Study on behalf of the European Commission.

Wik-Consult. 2005. *Evaluation des Schweizer Postmarktes*. Study on behalf of PostReg.

Wik-Consult. 2006. *Main developments Main Developments in the European Postal Sector (2004 – 2006)*. Study on behalf of the European Commission.

Wright, Julian. 2004. *One-sided Logic in Two-sided Markets*. Review of Network Economics Vol.3(1).

Die VDM Verlagsservicegesellschaft sucht für wissenschaftliche Verlage abgeschlossene und herausragende

Dissertationen, Habilitationen, Diplomarbeiten, Master Theses, Magisterarbeiten usw.

für die kostenlose Publikation als Fachbuch.

Sie verfügen über eine Arbeit, die hohen inhaltlichen und formalen Ansprüchen genügt, und haben Interesse an einer honorarvergüteten Publikation?

Dann senden Sie bitte erste Informationen über sich und Ihre Arbeit per Email an *info@vdm-vsg.de*.

Sie erhalten kurzfristig unser Feedback!

VDM Verlagsservicegesellschaft mbH
Dudweiler Landstr. 99   Telefon +49 681 3720 174
D - 66123 Saarbrücken   Fax   +49 681 3720 1749
www.vdm-vsg.de

Die VDM Verlagsservicegesellschaft mbH vertritt

Printed by Books on Demand GmbH, Norderstedt / Germany